WORLD HISTORY

The Women's Movement

Don Nardo

LUCENT BOOKS
A part of Gale, Cengage Learning

GALE
CENGAGE Learning

Detroit • New York • San Francisco • New Haven, Conn • Waterville, Maine • London

LIBRARY OF CONGRESS CATALOGING-IN-PUBLICATION DATA

Nardo, Don, 1947-
  The women's movement / by Don Nardo.
     p. cm. -- (World history)
  Includes bibliographical references and index.
  ISBN 978-1-4205-0592-4 (hardcover)
  1. Feminism--United States. 2. Women's rights--United States.
  3. Women--Suffrage--United States. I. Title.
   HQ1410.N365 2011
   305.420973--dc22

                                                                  2010050808

Lucent Books
27500 Drake Rd.
Farmington Hills, MI 48331

ISBN-13: 978-1-4205-0592-4
ISBN-10: 1-4205-0592-0

Printed in the United States of America
1 2 3 4 5 6 7 15 14 13 12 11
Printed by Bang Printing, Brainerd, MN, 1st Ptg., 04/2011

Contents

Foreword

Each year, on the first day of school, nearly every history teacher faces the task of explaining why his or her students should study history. Many reasons have been given. One is that lessons exist in the past from which contemporary society can benefit and learn. Another is that exploration of the past allows us to see the origins of our customs, ideas, and institutions. Concepts such as democracy, ethnic conflict, or even things as trivial as fashion or mores have historical roots.

Reasons such as these impress few students, however. If anything, these explanations seem remote and dull to young minds. Yet history is anything but dull. And therein lies what is perhaps the most compelling reason for studying history: History is filled with great stories. The classic themes of literature and drama—love and sacrifice, hatred and revenge, injustice and betrayal, adversity and overcoming adversity—fill the pages of history books, feeding the imagination as well as any of the great works of fiction do.

The story of the Children's Crusade, for example, is one of the most tragic in history. In 1212 Crusader fever hit Europe. A call went out from the pope that all good Christians should journey to Jerusalem to drive out the hated Muslims and return the city to Christian control. Heeding the call, thousands of children made the journey. Parents bravely allowed many children to go, and entire communities were inspired by the faith of these small Crusaders. Unfortunately, many who boarded ships were captained by slave traders, who enthusiastically sold the children into slavery as soon as they arrived at their destination. Thousands died from disease, exposure, and starvation on the long march across Europe to the Mediterranean Sea. Others perished at sea.

Another story, from a modern and more familiar place, offers a soul-wrenching view of personal humiliation but also the ability to rise above it. Hatsuye Egami was one of 110,000 Japanese Americans sent to internment camps during World War II. "Since yesterday we Japanese have ceased to be human beings," he wrote in his diary. "We are numbers. We are no longer Egamis, but the number 23324. A tag with that number is on every trunk, suitcase and bag. Tags, also, on our breasts." Despite such dehumanizing treatment, most internees worked hard to control their bitterness. They created workable communities inside the camps and demonstrated again and again their loyalty as Americans.

These are but two of the many stories from history that can be found in the pages of the Lucent Books World History series. All World History titles rely on sound research and verifiable evidence, and all give students a clear sense of time, place, and chronology through maps and timelines as well as text.

All titles include a wide range of authoritative perspectives that demonstrate the complexity of historical interpretation and sharpen the reader's critical thinking skills. Formally documented quotations and annotated bibliographies enable students to locate and evaluate sources, often instantaneously via the Internet, and serve as valuable tools for further research and debate.

Finally, Lucent's World History titles present rousing good stories, featuring vivid primary source quotations drawn from unique, sometimes obscure sources such as diaries, public records, and contemporary chronicles. In this way, the voices of participants and witnesses as well as important biographers and historians bring the study of history to life. As we are caught up in the lives of others, we are reminded that we too are characters in the ongoing human saga, and we better prepare for our own roles.

Important Dates at the Time

1848
Female rights activists organize the first regional U.S. women's conference, the Seneca Falls Convention.

1929
The U.S. stock market crashes, setting off a chain reaction that brings on the Great Depression.

1920
Congress passes the Nineteenth Amendment to the U.S. Constitution, giving women the right to vote.

1932
Hattie Caraway from Arkansas is the first woman to be elected to the U.S. Senate.

1894
Japan invades China and annexes Korea.

1850   1875   1900   1925   1950

1862
During the American Civil War, nurse Clara Barton enters the midst of battle to help wounded soldiers.

1939–1945
World War II rages, drawing in countries around the globe and killing more than 50 million people.

1950
An estimated 25 percent of American women are working outside the home.

1911
The Triangle Shirtwaist Company in New York City is destroyed by fire, killing 146 women.

of the Women's Movement

1961
President John F. Kennedy forms a special commission to find out how women are faring in society.

1975
U.S. military forces depart Vietnam after being defeated by local Communist troops.

1982
The Equal Rights Amendment, passed by Congress in 1972, fails to be ratified by the states.

2001
Terrorists attack the World Trade Center towers in New York City and the Pentagon in Washington, D.C.

1960	1970	1980	1990	2000

1966
Feminist Betty Friedan establishes the National Organization for Women to lobby for women's rights.

1964
The Palestine Liberation Organization, dedicated to fighting Israel, forms in the Middle East.

1992
In the so-called Year of the Woman, many U.S. women are elected to public offices across the country.

2008
Hillary Rodham Clinton is the first woman to win a U.S. presidential primary.

2010
President Barack Obama signs a new law that makes it easier for women to fight wage inequities in the workplace.

Working Toward the American Dream

Between the European settlement of North America in the 1600s and today, American women experienced an incredible transformation. They progressed from the status of second-class citizens with virtually no political or social rights to virtual equality with men, under the law. Their slow but steady march toward equality is often called the "women's movement." That term, along with formal writings about and studies of women's history and social progress, are all fairly recent phenomena. Indeed, only in the last fifty years or so was it even possible to read a book such as this one on the women's movement. Before that almost no books or essays existed to chronicle the struggles and achievements of American women as a social class.

This enormous inequity becomes more understandable when one takes even a brief look at the evolution of American women's education. For more than two centuries, the lack of organized, easily obtainable information about women's history mirrored or paralleled women's inadequate educational opportunities. In fact, only when women began to receive educations comparable to men's did systematic studies of women's history start to emerge.

Early Female Education

At first, little or no education for young women existed in colonial America, except for what they learned from their parents in the home. Typically a mother taught her daughter to cook, spin and weave, make clothes, and tend to other traditional "women's duties." In addition, a few colonial girls were fortunate enough to have their parents teach them reading and writing. Usually, however, literate women had few opportunities to use these skills, as society tended to frown on women expressing themselves in public, including in writing.

With some minor exceptions, the state of women's education remained this way for nearly two centuries.

Opportunities for female learning finally began increasing, though at first very slowly, in the 1800s. The first public school for girls opened in Worcester, Massachusetts, in 1824. There, and in similar schools that appeared in other states, the students learned basic skills, usually called the "three Rs" (standing for "reading, 'riting, and 'rithmetic"). As the number of elementary schools multiplied, calls were heard for schools of higher learning for young women. In

Educational opportunities for young girls in colonial times rarely went beyond how to do household chores, including cooking, spinning, and weaving. Few girls were taught to read and write.

answer to those calls, in 1837 Oberlin College in Ohio became the country's first institute of higher learning to admit both men and women.

Initially, however, the courses offered to women at such colleges were shorter and less complex than those offered to men. This was partly because the prevailing wisdom was that women's brains were incapable of assimilating as much knowledge as men's. Also, the administrators and teachers at Oberlin and similar schools did not expect or desire their female graduates to go on to take the kind of high-profile jobs traditionally performed by men. Scholar Robert S. Fletcher explains how some men felt about education for women:

> If women became lawyers, ministers, physicians, lecturers, politicians, or any sort of "public character," the home would suffer from neglect. . . . Washing the men's clothes, caring for their rooms, serving them at table, listening to their orations, but themselves [that is, women] remaining respectfully silent in public assemblages, the Oberlin "co-eds" were being prepared for intelligent motherhood and a properly subservient wifehood.[1]

This condescending attitude toward women and their social place slowly but steadily changed during the late 1800s and early 1900s. Over time it was increasingly seen as desirable for some women to become teachers, caretakers, or social workers, for example. That allowed them to make important inroads into the workforce. It also stimulated the creation of more schools for women or for both women and men. By the early 1900s roughly 70 percent of colleges and universities were coeducational, and about 30 percent of their students were women. Moreover, they started taking the same courses as the men.

Nevertheless, these institutions still discriminated against women by employing quota systems. As one modern expert explains:

> Across higher education, quotas restricted women's access. Under Stanford [University]'s quota system, three males were accepted for every female. Histories of higher education reveal other uses of quotas. For many years there were quotas for Jews. Jewish women faced an at least double barrier, gender and religion, as did white ethnic working-class women who were not only limited by gender and poverty, but in some cases also by their Catholicism. Even when prestigious private men's universities opened their doors to women, admissions quotas were again set.[2]

Mounting Opportunities for Women

Fortunately for women seeking to better themselves, these quotas were removed as the twentieth century progressed. However, women attending colleges and universities still could not study about their own history in the courses offered in these schools. The historical narrative of women in America was ignored in both college curricula and virtually all U.S. history texts. In 1922 the American historian Arthur M. Schlesinger called attention to this glaring oversight, saying: "Any consideration of woman's part in American history must include the protracted [long and drawn out] struggle of the sex for larger rights and opportunities, a story that is in itself one of the noblest chapters in the history of American democracy."[3]

To rectify what many people saw as an inexcusable situation, in the years that followed, scholars of both genders tackled the difficult task of writing accounts of women's historical experiences and struggles. One of the earliest successful examples was Abbie Graham's *Ladies in Revolt*, penned in 1934. But studies of women's history really began to come of age in 1959, when three landmark books were published. One, Eleanor Flexner's *Century of Struggle: The Women's Rights Movement in the United States*, was the first comprehensive history of the nineteenth-century women's movement. In periodic updated versions, it remains one of the most important available books about women's history. The other two important works about women first released in 1959 were *A Century of Higher Education for American Women* by Mabel Newcomer and *Women and Work in America* by Robert Smuts.

These milestones were followed by a flood of books about women's his-

Women gather in Vermont to bring attention to the issue of equal pay for equal work, which remains one of the goals of the women's movement.

tory, stimulated in large degree by an upsurge of interest in social and family history that began in the 1960s. This soon led to the emergence of "women's studies" programs in colleges and universities. Before 1969 no such programs existed in the United States except for a few single courses on women's history. By the early 1990s, in contrast, more than five hundred women's studies programs existed, most of which offered a major or minor degree. Scholar Elizabeth L. Kennedy describes the major goals of these programs:

The content of women's studies came to include identifying and criticizing male bias in research and curriculum; encouraging teaching and research about women and gender; and using this new knowledge to develop women-centered but inclusive frameworks for understanding the world. Such a comprehensive definition of women's studies encouraged its development in social sciences, natural sciences, education, the law, and the humanities.[4]

Throughout the twentieth century, the growing opportunities for women to become well educated and the increase of books and other resources examining women's history went hand in hand with the growth of feminism. Feminism is an organized, ongoing attempt by women to acquire social, political, and other rights equal to those of men. All of these aspects of women's lives—education, historical studies, and the fight for rights—have complemented and strengthened one another. Together feminists have worked and continue to work toward the day when all women are fully equal with men. In the words of University of Minnesota scholar Sara M. Evans, American women seek no special treatment, but rather only to "claim for themselves the status of full participants in the construction of the American dream."[5]

Chapter One

The Ordeal of Early American Women

Women's fight for complete equality with men in America, which is still ongoing, goes back several centuries. From the very beginning of America, in early colonial times, women were relegated to second-class status, legally, politically, and socially. Although upper-class women were viewed as socially superior to women, and men too, of the lower classes, no woman had the right to vote or run for political office. Also, every woman was legally inferior to her husband, brother, or father. In short, colonial men had expansive rights, and colonial women had almost none. With some minor improvements and advances, women's second-class status continued for several decades following the American Revolution and creation of the infant United States.

Women Subject to Men

The attitude of the vast majority of colonial men toward women was summed up by John Winthrop, leader of the Puritans in the 1630s and longtime governor of the Massachusetts Bay Colony. Feeling that men should maintain strict control over women, he said:

He [the husband] is her [the wife's] lord and she is to be subject to him, yet in a way of liberty, not of bondage, and a true wife accounts her subjection, her honor, and freedom, and would not think her condition safe and free but in her subjection to her husband's authority. Such is the liberty of the church under the authority of Christ, her king and husband. His yoke is so easy and sweet to her as a bride's ornaments. And if through forwardness and wantonness, etc., she shakes it [her husband's authority] off at any time, she is at no rest in her spirit until she takes it up again. And whether her lord smiles upon her and embraces her in his arms, or rebukes [rejects] or smites [strikes] her, she apprehends the sweetness of his love.[6]

As a result of this superior male attitude, which was commonplace in that historical period, women had no legal rights to speak of. A married woman in late seventeenth-century America could not sign contracts. Nor could she keep and spend her own earnings (if she had a job, which was rare), or sell property, even if she had inherited it. Moreover, a woman could not acquire custody of her children if she and her

Puritan leader John Winthrop expressed his belief that women should willingly submit to their husband's authority. This was a prevailing attitude during the early colonial era.

husband were legally separated. As for divorce, a woman could get one only in the most extreme circumstances—if her husband deserted her or beat her brutally on a regular basis. (A moderate amount of abuse of women was socially accepted.) Men often used religion to rationalize this nearly complete domination of women. "The colonists might be dissenters of one kind or another against the Church of England," the late, distinguished scholar Eleanor Flexner explained,

> but they were at one with it in believing that women's place was determined by limitations of mind and body, a punishment for the original sin of Eve. However, in order to fit her for her proper role of motherhood, the Almighty had taken especial pains to endow her with such virtues as modesty, meekness, compassion, affability [friendliness], and piety.[7]

Another notable aspect of early American women's second-class social status was that often they were not allowed to marry the men of their choice. This was partly because maintaining existing social ranks, or classes, was seen as imperative. As in most societies throughout history, a small group of well-to-do individuals made up society's upper class, while the bulk of the population was made up of folks of limited means. The rich and powerful naturally desired to preserve the status quo, in which they dominated

A painting depicts a Puritan husband and wife. During that era, women had no legal rights and were usually not allowed to marry the men of their choice.

the lower classes. So for a woman to marry outside her social rank was frowned on and even forbidden by many fathers. One of those fathers, a Virginia aristocrat named William Byrd II, left behind the following diary entry expressing his condemnation of

Education Determines Male Advantages?

During the American Revolution, a Massachusetts woman named Judith Thompson wrote an essay (not published until after the war) in which she made the point that men appear smarter than women only because males are better educated.

Is it indeed a fact that [nature] has yielded to one half the human species so unquestionable a mental superiority? . . . Yet it may be questioned, from what source does this superiority, in its determining factor of the soul (the judgment), proceed? May we not trace its source in the difference of education and continued advantages [enjoyed by men]? Will it be said that the judgment of a male two years old is more sage [wise] than that of a female's of the same age? I believe the reverse is generally observed to be true. But [as the years proceed] how is the [male] exalted and the [female] depressed by the contrary modes of education that are adopted! The [male] is taught to aspire, the [female] is early confined and limited. As their years increase, the sister must be wholly domesticated, while the brother is led by the hand through all the flowery paths of science.

Constantia [Judith Thompson], "The Equality of the Sexes," *Massachusetts Magazine*, March/April, 1790, pp. 132–33.

an upper-class young woman who had married a lower-class man:

I learned all the tragic story of [the young woman's] humble marriage with her uncle's overseer. Besides the meanness [lowliness] of this mortal's aspect [condition], the man has not one visible qualification, except impudence, to recommend him to a [decent] female. . . . Had she run away with a gentleman or a pretty fellow, there might have been some excuse for her, though he were of inferior fortune. But to stoop to a dirty plebian [low-class person], without any kind of merit is the lowest [kind of] prostitution.[8]

Relentless, Grinding Toil

In addition to their plight as second-class citizens, colonial women endured lives filled with physically difficult and exhausting duties that they could not avoid. Married women were not the only females who faced this harsh reality. A large proportion of the women who came to North America in the 1600s were unmarried indentured servants. They were expected to work a set number of years for the man who paid their way across the ocean. According to historian David F. Hawke, such a servile woman was legally bound

to serve out her indenture, and since the law forbade a servant to marry until she had completed her contract, that meant four or five years must pass before she could get a husband. They were devastating years. Exposure to malaria left her susceptible to more deadly diseases. The physical work was harder than anything she had known in England. If she served a small planter, she had, in addition to household chores, the fields to tend. She was easily exploited and degraded, for on an isolated farm there were few effective checks to the authority of the planter or his often shrewish wife. . . . If the woman lived through her service, a quick marriage was inevitable in a land where men outnumbered women seven to one.[9]

Even after single women did marry, their lives were no less filled with what would be seen today as relentless, grinding toil. One expert on colonial women writes:

The labor of the colonial housewife was backbreaking drudgery. In a frontier settlement, housekeeping was only part of her duties. She helped to clear the land and build the house and plant the crops as

well. Even when she lived in a village of snug, comfortable houses, her daily tasks filled every hour from sunrise to long after sunset.[10]

Housework, yard work, and agricultural labor were not the only duties that sapped the strength and tested the resolve of early American women. The very fact that they were women made them society's child bearers whether they liked it or not. Moreover, they did not have an average of just two to three children per household. Rather, most colonia-era women had many children. The causes of disease were not yet known, and medicine was still a primitive art. Thus, infant mortality rates were so high that four out of ten children born in Britain's American colonies were dead before the age of six. It was therefore common for couples to have eight, twelve, or even fourteen or more children. That created a tremendous physical strain on the health of large numbers of women. The average colonial woman's long list of daily, weekly, and seasonal duties included keeping track of and disciplining a houseful of children of varying ages while at the same time enduring the physical effects of a subsequent pregnancy.

In addition to their many physical tasks and obligations, some early colonial women were also the targets of mean-spirited prejudices, superstitions, and suspicions of criminal acts because of a lingering belief in witches. The most famous example of such prejudice took place in Salem, Massachusetts, in the

A painting depicts a woman thought to be a witch being tortured in Salem, Massachusetts. Witch trials in the 1690s resulted in the arrest of hundreds.

1690s. A few young girls in that town began having strange and sometimes violent fits. Several adults then jumped to the conclusion that the girls' bizarre behavior was caused by witches. At the time most people still believed that witches, along with sorcery, demons, and so forth, were real. The result was one of the best documented cases of mass hysteria in modern history. Gripped by fear, neighbors accused one another of being witches, and the authorities put numerous local residents, mostly women, on trial for practicing witchcraft. Hundreds of townspeople went to jail, and at least twenty were executed before the hysteria ran its course.

Education the Key

Opportunities for women to escape both their unrelenting physical labor and the prejudices against them were extremely limited. Over time it became clear that education was the key, not only for men but also for women, to improving one's lot in life. The problem for women, however, was that at first, little or no educational opportunities existed for them, with occasional exceptions. The Puritans of Massachusetts Bay, for instance, strongly emphasized learning and did allow some women to be taught reading and writing. One of them, Anne Bradstreet, enjoyed the distinction of being the first female American to become published. Part of one of her poems, titled "To My Dear and Loving Husband," reads:

My love is such that rivers cannot
   quench,
Nor ought but love from thee give
   recompense.
Thy love is such I can no way
   repay.
The heavens reward thee manifold,
   I pray.
Then while we live, in love let's so
   persevere
That when we live no more, we
   may live ever.[11]

These words reveal that true love did exist between early colonial men and women. It is unclear, though, whether the poet's gratitude for being allowed to express herself in writing, a right possessed by few women at the time, accounted for some of her fond feelings for her husband. In any case most women in the 1600s, and even in the 1700s, could not read or write. They received no formal education, in part because most men felt they were not worthy of it. The famous eighteenth-century thinker and writer Jean-Jacques Rousseau stated the prevailing male attitude toward educating women. Namely, females' primary role was to support the male of the species and make men's lives more pleasant:

The whole education of women ought to be relative to men. To please them, to be useful to them, to make themselves loved and honored by them, to educate them when young, to care for them when grown, to counsel them, to console them, and to make life sweet and agreeable to them—these are the duties of women at all times, and what should be taught them from their infancy.[12]

American women of Rousseau's time were in no position to write and publish rebuttals to such writings. So it was not until 1818 that a female Bostonian essayist, Hannah Mather Crocker, responded to Rousseau's position on women's education. In her book *Observations on the Real Rights of Women*, she states: "There can be no doubt, but [that] there is as much difference in the powers of each individual of the male sex as there is of the female [sex], and if [women] received the same mode of education [as men do], their [personal and social] improvement would be fully equal."[13]

Early Schools for Women

That Crocker was able to reach at least a small audience of readers in the early 1800s demonstrates that the idea of formal education for women was beginning to gain steam. Indeed, only a year after her book appeared, New York governor DeWitt Clinton came out in support of an educational project proposed to him by Emma Willard, the wife of a Vermont physician. Willard wanted to establish a seminary, then meaning a private secondary school, for girls in their teens. The New York legislature approved the school's charter, and the town of Troy put up the money to build it. In 1821 the Troy Female Seminary became the first secondary, or preparatory, school (today called a high school) for young women in the United States. The students took courses in history, science, geography, and other subjects taught in secondary men's schools.

It must be emphasized that Willard's school was private and required the girls to pay tuition (about two hundred dollars per year, then seen as a considerable sum). Most of the girls who attended it and other secondary schools that appeared in the years that followed came from well-to-do families. Their parents were able to afford to hire tutors for them in their grade school, or elementary, years. Or the parents themselves taught them basic skills that prepared them for secondary school. Otherwise, the few secondary schools for girls that existed at the time had no sources of new students. This was because before the 1820s the country had only a tiny handful of free, or public, schools for children and none admitted girls. The first public school for girls opened in 1824 in Worcester, Massachusetts, and another appeared in New York City two years later.

Soon afterward, a movement to create public schools for girls gained momentum thanks to the efforts of a new generation of women writers who felt that women's social status should be equal to that of men. Among them was Scottish-born Frances Wright, often called Fanny Wright. Beginning in the late 1820s, she argued that women should achieve educations comparable to men's. That, she said, would be a crucial step in women's quest for social equality. Wright argued that women's equality was essential for a moral and advanced society because treating women as inferiors actually degraded the status and worth of men. She stated:

> It is in vain that we would circumscribe [restrict] the power of one half of our race, and that half by far the most important and influential. . . . If they advance not knowledge, they will perpetuate ignorance. Let women stand where they may in the scale of improvement. Their position decides that of the [human] race. Are they [women] cultivated? [If] so, society [is] polished and enlightened. Are they ignorant? [If] so, it [is] gross and insipid [bland]. Are they wise? [If] so, the human condition [is] pros-

perous. Are they foolish? [If] so, it [is] unstable and unpromising. Are they free? [If] so, the human character [is] elevated. Are they enslaved? [If] so, the whole race [is] degraded. Oh! that we could learn the advantage of just practice and consistent principles! . . . Equality is the soul of liberty. There is, in fact, no liberty without it.[14]

These words were only a small part of one of the lectures Wright delivered in New York, Philadelphia, Boston, Baltimore, and other U.S. cities in the 1830s and 1840s. Many of those who attended were women. But quite often she spoke to audiences of men as well. Some men viewed her as a dangerous radical out to ruin traditional society. Others, however, thought that her arguments made good sense, and as a result her social influence grew over the years. The right of women to receive a decent education, along with the larger cause of women's social equality, advanced significantly, thanks to her tireless efforts. These accomplishments inspired a later activist for women's rights, Ernestine L. Rose, to declare in 1858:

Frances Wright was the first woman in this country who spoke on the equality of the sexes. She had indeed a hard task before her. The elements [existing social attitudes]

A Founding Mother Pleads for Equality

In March 1776 Abigail Adams, wife of patriot and future U.S. president John Adams, wrote to him asking that, when he and his colleagues met to form a new nation, they would please remember women's desire for greater rights and autonomy.

In the new code of laws which I suppose it will be necessary for you to make, I desire you would remember the ladies and be more generous and favorable to them than your ancestors. Do not put such unlimited power into the hands of the husbands. Remember, all men would be tyrants if they could. If particular care and attention is not paid to the ladies, we are determined to foment a rebellion, and will not hold ourselves bound by any laws in which we have no voice or representation. That your sex are naturally tyrannical is a truth so thoroughly established as to admit of no dispute. . . . Regard us then as being placed by Providence [God or fate] under your protection, [and] make use of that power only for our happiness.

Quoted in "Letters Between Abigail Adams and Her Husband John Adams," Liz Library. www .thelizlibrary.org/suffrage/abigail.htm.

Scottish-born activist Frances Wright argued that educational opportunities were key to women achieving social equality.

were entirely unprepared. She had to break up the time-hardened soil of conservatism [traditional values and beliefs], and her reward was sure—the same reward that is always bestowed upon those who are in the vanguard of any great movement. She was subjected to public odium [hatred], slander, and persecution. But these were not the only things she received. Oh, she had her reward, that reward of which no enemies could deprive her, which no slanders could make less precious—the eternal reward of knowing that she had done her duty.[15]

A Safer, More Dignified Profession?

Even as the barriers against elementary and secondary schools for young women were breaking, women's rights activists were working to establish schools of higher learning for women.

Oberlin College, which was founded in Ohio in 1833, began admitting women a few years later. The first female to take a full schedule of courses there graduated in 1841. Soon afterward Oberlin awarded a degree to Lucy Stone, who went on to become one of the nation's leading orators. One of her fellow graduates, Antoinette Brown, became the first woman in the United States to be ordained a minister.

In this same period, an educator and women's rights activist named Catherine Beecher appeared on the scene. As a young woman in the late 1820s, she

Standing Up for the "Tender Sex"

Not all men in colonial times viewed women as inferiors. One who condemned their plight as second-class citizens was U.S. founding father Thomas Paine, who stated in 1775:

If we take a survey of ages and of countries, we shall find the women, almost—without exception—at all times and in all places, adored and oppressed. Man, who has never neglected an opportunity of exerting his power, in paying homage to their beauty, has always availed himself of their weakness. He has been at once their tyrant and their slave. . . . Even in countries where they may be esteemed most happy, constrained in their desires in the disposal of their goods, robbed of freedom of will by the laws, the slaves of opinion, which rules them with absolute sway, and construes [interprets] the slightest appearances into guilt; surrounded on all sides by judges, who are at once tyrants and their seducers, and who, after having prepared their faults, punish every lapse with dishonor—nay, usurp the right of degrading them on suspicion! Who does not feel for the tender sex? Yet such, I am sorry to say, is the lot of women over the whole earth.

Thomas Paine, "An Occasional Letter on the Female Sex," *Pennsylvania Magazine*, August 1775, Classical Liberals, p. 363. http://classicliberal.tripod.com/paine/fmlsx.html.

Abolitionist and suffragist Lucy Stone earned a degree from Oberlin College in 1847. Oberlin was the first university in the United States to admit women.

had run a small secondary school for girls in Connecticut. In time, Beecher became increasingly concerned that young women get good educations. In the 1830s tens of thousands of young men from the East, searching for adventure or better lives, headed for the Midwest and West. Those who were married took their wives with them or sent for them later. But many of these men were unmarried. So that drained the existing pool of prospective husbands for single women in the East, leaving large numbers of young women unmarried and needing to support themselves.

A large proportion of these women took jobs in factories in eastern manufacturing towns like Lowell, Massachusetts. By the early 1850s, Lowell had the largest manufacturing complex in the country and employed many thousands of women, most of them single. In such factories in eastern towns, women worked long hours for little pay and often endured unsanitary and/or dangerous working conditions.

It would be better, Beecher said, if more women who needed jobs became teachers. In her view, one shared by growing numbers of women and even a few men, teaching was a safer, more dignified profession. (She also promoted the idea of women becoming nurses and child-care professionals.) As a result, Beecher developed a plan for building a chain of "normal schools," colleges to train teachers, in the Midwest. One of the schools she helped to make a reality—Milwaukee-Downer College in Wisconsin—is still in operation today. To rally support for her plan, in 1852 Beecher founded the American Women's Educational Association. Later generations came to see her as one of the "founding mothers" of modern teachers' training.

Besides providing thousands of women with paying jobs, another outcome of Beecher's work was that teaching became a respected profession dominated by women. For the first time, large numbers of American women could work outside the home in a job that required an education comparable to that of the average educated man. Also, teaching was a profession in which women principally used their minds and personal talents, as opposed to breaking their backs and spirits doing unrelenting physical labor.

In this way, the first major barrier to female social equality in the United States was shattered. Many success-ful female teachers, nurses, and other professional women of that era affectionately remembered a passage from one of Frances Wright's more popular lectures. "However novel it may appear," she declared, "I shall venture the assertion that, until women assume the place in society which good sense and good feeling alike assign to them, human improvement must advance but feebly."[16]

Chapter Two

Women Learn How to Organize

Even as women's educational opportunities expanded in the 1830s and 1840s, their struggles for social equality began to gain energy and notoriety. During this period the women's movement received both inspiration and a major boost from another movement—abolitionism. The fight to abolish slavery became an increasingly large and contentious issue in the three decades preceding the American Civil War (1861–1865). Large numbers of women took part in abolitionist activities. Most of them saw a natural parallel between racial equality and gender equality and felt justified in supporting the fight for women's rights along with the battle to end slavery. In the words of a prominent expert on the women's movement:

> Thousands of men and women were drawn into the [antislavery] work. Among the latter were the first conscious feminists, who would go to school in the struggle to free the slaves and, in the process, launch their own fight for equality. It was in the abolition movement that women first learned to organize, to hold public meetings, to conduct petition campaigns. As abolitionists they first won the right to speak in public, and began to evolve a philosophy of their place in society and of their basic rights. For a quarter of a century the two movements, to free the slave and liberate the woman, nourished and strengthened each other.[17]

Slaves' Cause Is Women's Cause

The abolitionist movement, which captured the hearts and minds of thousands of American women and taught them how to organize themselves, first began in England and France in the late 1700s. As it gained momentum, it spread across the Atlantic to the recently established United States. At first the abolitionists aimed their attacks on the Atlantic slave trade. In a growing torrent of books, newspaper articles, and public speeches, they condemned the buying and selling of human beings. Abolitionists also convinced many religious leaders to join the cause, which gave the movement more weight in the minds of many people. The result of these efforts was impressive. In 1807 Britain banned the slave trade and the importation of black Africans into its territories worldwide. The United States followed suit in the following year.

Yet these victories over injustice marked only the beginning of the abolitionist movement. In the decades that followed, it began to target the slavery institution itself and set the daunting goal of wiping it out for good. Although some American men became abolitionists, considerable numbers of American women were drawn to the cause. Because women were treated as social inferiors themselves, many of them sympathized with the plight of black slaves. Female abolitionists also recognized early on that winning the fight against slavery could earn them increased respect and make them a social and political force to be reckoned with. As scholar Shirley J. Yee puts it, "The fact that abolitionists were already wrestling with the issue of racial equality as a goal of the movement created a climate ripe for discussions of equality between the sexes."[18]

The result was that at first hundreds and later many thousands of women threw themselves into antislavery activities. They included both whites and free Northern blacks. One prominent black abolitionist was Philadelphia's Grace Bustill Douglass, who helped to establish the biracial Philadelphia Female Anti-Slavery Society in 1833. Her daughter Sarah Douglass spent more than forty years fighting for educational opportunities for African American children, both male and female. Another noted black female abolitionist, Harriet Tubman, was born a slave and eventually escaped from a Maryland plantation. She courageously returned to the South several times to help free hundreds of slaves and lead them to safety in the North.

One of the more prominent white female abolitionists was Lucretia Coffin Mott. She and her husband, James, were among the leaders of the Free Produce Movement, which employed the tactic of boycotting goods produced by Southern slaves, especially cotton. Two other white antislavery activists, sisters Sarah and Angelina Grimke of South Carolina, tirelessly traveled through the North giving speeches denouncing slavery. They also consistently linked the issues of slaves' freedom and women's equality. Some men in the movement asked them to stop talking about women's rights because they felt it diluted the antislavery message. But they refused to stop. "If we surrender

Harriet Tubman escaped from slavery and joined the abolitionists' cause, personally leading hundreds of slaves to safety via the Underground Railroad. Later in life, she was an advocate for women's suffrage.

the right to *speak* in public this year," Angelina told the men, "we must surrender the right to petition next year, and the right to *write* the year after, and so on. What *then* can *women* do for the slave, when she herself is under the fear of man and shamed into *silence?*"[19]

Although thousands of other women played important roles in the abolitionist movement, none had a bigger ultimate impact against slavery than Harriet Beecher Stowe. The daughter of a Northern minister, in 1852 she published *Uncle Tom's Cabin*. It was the fictional story of a virtuous Christian slave named Tom who is viciously beaten to death by his brutal master. Stowe's book became an enormous best seller and persuaded large numbers of Americans to support the abolition of slavery. When President Abraham Lincoln met Stowe later, during the Civil War, he supposedly quipped: "So you're the little woman who wrote the book that made this great war."[20]

Overall, the contribution that women lecturers, writers, and other activists made to the antislavery movement was central to its eventual success. The famous African American writer and abolitionist Frederick Douglass paid tribute to that contribution. "When the true history of the anti-slavery cause

shall be written," he said, "women will occupy a large space in its pages, for the cause of the slave has been peculiarly women's cause. Her heart and her conscience have supplied in large degree its motive and mainspring."[21]

"Man Cannot Speak for Us"

Some of the courageous and hardworking women Douglass had spoken so highly of felt that they could not wait until slavery was eliminated to begin organizing a movement for their own

Abolitionist Harriet Beecher Stowe wrote Uncle Tom's Cabin, *a fictionalized tale of slave life published in 1852. The book became a best seller and furthered the antislavery cause.*

rights. Two who decided to act on that feeling were the Free Produce Movement's Lucretia Mott and her friend Elizabeth Cady Stanton, who was also close to the Grimke sisters.

Mott and Stanton had first met at the World Anti-Slavery Convention in London in 1840. Caught up in the excitement of that huge gathering of educated, passionate people, they discussed the idea of organizing a similar meeting for the advancement of women. But several years passed before they were both in a position to transform their idea into reality.

In the early summer of 1848, Mott, Stanton, and three other women, Jane Hunt, Martha Wright, and Mary Ann McClintock, met in Waterloo, New York, near Seneca Falls. They committed themselves to launching a movement for women's rights. Then they drafted an announcement to advertise the event, which appeared in the July 4 issue of the *Seneca County Courier* and read:

Women's Rights Convention—A convention to discuss the social, civil, and religious rights of women will be held in the Wesleyan Cha-

To Remedy the Wrongs of Society

Elizabeth Cady Stanton, one of the organizers of the Seneca Falls Convention, spent much of her marriage alone while her husband was away on business. She eventually wrote about one of her motives in the struggle for women's rights—the difficulties of taking care of a house and children by herself.

I now fully understood the practical difficulties most women had to contend with in the isolated household, and the impossibility of woman's best development if in contact, the chief part of her life, [only] with servants and children. The general discontent I felt with woman's portion as wife, mother, housekeeper, physical, and spiritual guide, the chaotic conditions into which everything fell without her supervision, and the wearied, anxious look of the majority of women impressed me with a strong feeling that some measures should be taken to remedy the wrongs of society in general and of women in particular. In this tempest-tossed condition of mind I received an invitation to spend the day with Lucretia Mott. At her house I poured out the torrent of my long-accumulating discontent. We decided, then and there, to call a "Woman's Rights Convention."

Elizabeth Cady Stanton, *Eighty Years and More*. New York: T. Fisher Unwin, 1898, p. 147.

pel, Seneca Falls, New York, on Wednesday and Thursday, the 19th and 20th of July current; commencing at 10 A.M. During the first day the meeting will be held exclusively for women, who are earnestly invited to attend. The public generally are invited to be present on the second day, when Lucretia Mott of Philadelphia and other ladies and gentlemen will address the convention.[22]

The meeting took place on the appointed days. To the organizers' surprise, despite the stipulation that women only should attend on the first day, forty men, including Frederick Douglass, showed up. They were graciously seated. Around 240 women also arrived, after which a long series of discussions and speeches ensued. One of the most emotional and memorable was given by Stanton. She said in part:

Abolitionist Elizabeth Cady Stanton had the idea of holding a meeting to address issues of women's equality several years before organizing the first Women's Rights Convention in Seneca Falls, New York, in July 1848.

The time [has] come for the question of women's wrongs to be laid before the public. [I believe] that woman herself must do this work, for woman alone can understand the height, the depth, the length, and the breadth of her degradation and woe. Man cannot speak for us—because he has been educated to believe that we differ from him so materially, that he cannot judge of our thoughts, feelings and opinions by his own. . . . Among the many important questions which have been brought before the public, there is none that more vitally affects the whole human family than that which is technically termed Woman's rights. Every allusion to the degraded and inferior position occupied by woman all over the world, has ever been met by scorn and abuse. [We here today] dare assert that woman stands by the side of man—his equal, placed here by her God to enjoy with him the beautiful earth, which is her home as it is his—having the same sense of right and wrong and looking to the same Being for guidance and support.[23]

At War with Mankind's Interests

In this excerpt from Elizabeth Cady Stanton's "Declaration of Sentiments and Resolutions," she stresses that women's equality with men is only part of nature's plan.

R esolved, therefore, that, being invested by the Creator with the same capabilities, and the same consciousness of responsibility for their exercise, it is demonstrably the right and duty of woman, equally with man, to promote every righteous cause, by every righteous mean, and especially in regard to the great subjects of morals and religion, it is self-evidently her right to participate with her brother in teaching them both in private and public. . . . And this being a self-evident truth, growing out of the divinely implanted principles of human nature, and custom or authority averse to it . . . is to be regarded as self-evident falsehood, and at war with the interests of mankind.

Quoted in Sally G. McMillen, *Seneca Falls and the Origins of the Women's Rights Movement*. New York: Oxford University Press, 2008, pp. 240–41.

A Movement Is Launched

The speech was not Stanton's only broadside against long-standing gender inequality. All who attended the gathering endorsed the ideas contained in a document that she had drafted a few days before. Called the "Declaration of Sentiments and Resolutions," it is couched in the style and format of the U.S. Declaration of Independence. For example, Stanton's tract begins:

When, in the course of human events, it becomes necessary for one portion of the family of man to assume among the people of the earth a position different from that which they have hitherto occupied, but one to which the laws of nature

and of nature's God entitle them, a decent respect to the opinions of mankind requires that they should declare the causes that impel them to such a course. We hold these truths to be self-evident: that all men and women are created equal; that they are endowed by their Creator with certain inalienable rights; that among these are life, liberty, and the pursuit of happiness.[24]

After establishing that women were originally created equal to men, Stanton's declaration lists some of the ways that men had established "an absolute tyranny" over women. These include denying them the right to vote, forcing them to submit to laws they had no say in creating, making it difficult if not impossible to obtain divorces, and taking from them "all right in property, even to the wages [we] earn." The document concludes with a series of resolutions. One states that all rules and laws that prevent women from enjoying the same social positions as men are invalid and have no authority. Also:

> Woman is man's equal [and] the highest good of the race demands that she should be recognized as such. Resolved, that the women of this country ought to be enlightened in regard to the laws under which they live, that they may no longer publish their degradation by declaring themselves satisfied with their present position, nor their ignorance, by asserting that they have all the rights they want.[25]

The organizers and attendees of the Seneca Falls Convention had high hopes that what they were doing would have positive results for women in the future. They did not imagine the immensity of the flood that would grow from the tiny trickle they had loosed. "A movement had been launched," the late historian Eleanor Flexner wrote, "that would leave its imprint on the lives of their daughters and of women throughout the world."[26]

Regional and National Conventions

Although the gathering that Stanton and her colleagues had organized would

definitely prove crucial in the history of the women's movement, the rights that they called for were still many years in the future. Indeed, only one of the 240 women present at the meeting, Charlotte Woodward, lived long enough to be allowed to vote. (She cast her ballot in the 1920 presidential election, shortly after women gained the right to vote.)

The reality that women in the late 1840s still had a long path to tread toward the liberty they sought was well illustrated by the events that occurred immediately following the Seneca Falls Convention. Only a day after that official birth of the modern women's rights movement, those who had attended the meeting found themselves the targets of mean-spirited male backlash. To ridicule the convention, several newspapers published the entire "Declaration of Sentiments and Resolutions" and included the names of the women who had signed it. Researchers Bonnie Eisenberg and Mary Ruthsdotter explain the unexpected consequences that followed:

> Just as ridicule today often has a squelching [stifling] effect on new ideas, this attack in the press caused many people from the Convention to rethink their positions. Many of the women who had attended . . . were so embarrassed by the publicity that they actually withdrew their signatures from the Declaration. But most stood firm. And something the editors had not anticipated happened. Their negative articles about the women's call

for expanded rights were so livid and widespread that they actually had a positive impact far beyond anything the organizers could have hoped for. People in cities and isolated towns alike were now alerted to the issues, and joined this heated discussion of women's rights in great numbers! The Seneca Falls women had optimistically hoped for a series of conventions embracing every part of the country. And that's just what did happen.[27]

In fact, so many regional gatherings of women took place that a national women's convention became inevitable. The first one occurred in 1850 in Worcester, Massachusetts. It was organized by many people, most notably Lucy Stone and Pauline Wright Davis. Lucy Stone, who had both money and connections in high places, presided as president at the convention. Her involvement in the movement helped it grow and attract a number of new, socially prominent members. Among them were America's first female ordained minister, Antoinette Brown; noted lecturer Elizabeth Oakes Smith; and the dynamic African American writer and lecturer Sojourner Truth. Between 1850 and 1860, national women's rights conventions were held in every year except 1857. Meanwhile, smaller regional and local gatherings took place in most of the Northern states.

An illustration shows a scene from a women's rights convention. Despite negative coverage in the press, the number of conventions increased on both the regional and national level throughout the 1850s.

During these years the press remained mostly hostile to women's efforts to achieve equal rights. "What do the leaders of the women's rights convention want?" one editor asked. Answering his own question, he went on, "They want to vote and hustle with the rowdies at the polls. They want to be members of Congress, and in the heat of debate subject themselves to coarse jests and indecent language."[28] Even more critical and scornful was a newspaper editorial that crudely reacted to the 1853 New York City Women's Rights Convention:

> We saw, in broad daylight, in a public hall in the city of New York, a gathering of unsexed women . . . publicly propounding the doctrine that they should be allowed to step out of their appropriate sphere, and mingle in the busy walks of everyday life, to the neglect of those duties which both human and divine law have assigned to them. [These] women are entirely devoid of personal attractions. They are generally thin maiden ladies [who] violate the rules of decency and taste by attiring themselves in eccentric [outfits], which hang loosely and inelegantly upon their forms, making [them] an object of aversion and disgust.[29]

Women in the Civil War

The women who attended the conventions and otherwise promoted women's rights reached a sort of crossroads at the outbreak of the Civil War in 1861. Some wanted to press on with their struggle for equality. But a great many others felt that they should put such efforts on hold during the conflict, an enormous event that to one degree or another affected the lives of nearly all Americans. The majority of women, therefore, white, black, Southerner, and Northerner alike, had two main goals during the hostilities. These were to ensure that they and their families survived and/or to aid in the war effort.

General reactions to the war by women were more or less the same regardless of where they lived and which side they were on. Mothers, wives, and daughters in both the South and North were highly patriotic, and most supported the political positions of their male relatives. In the South, for example, where the states seceded (withdrew) from the Union and formed the Confederacy, many women expected or even demanded that their husbands or sons join the army. When her fiancé did not run off to enlist, an Alabama woman broke off their engagement and challenged his masculinity by giving him a skirt to wear. In the North, meanwhile, a New York woman reacted to the outbreak of fighting by saying, "It seems as if we never were alive till now [and] never had a country till now."[30] No less zealous was Louisa May Alcott, author of the novel *Little Women*, who said, "I long to be a man. But as I can't fight, I will content myself with working for those who can."[31]

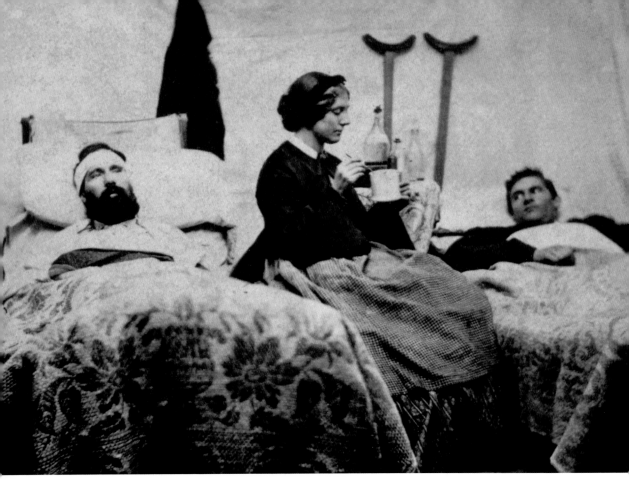

A nurse tends to two injured Union soldiers in a field hospital during the Civil War. Women made numerous contributions to the war effort on both sides of the conflict.

Alcott was far from alone in wishing she could fight like the men did. Historians have documented at least 240 cases of women, both Northerners and Southerners, disguising themselves as men and fighting alongside male soldiers. Larger numbers of women chose to help the troops by taking over a wide range of jobs. Many ran family farms or businesses while their husbands were away fighting. Others served as clerks in government offices, postal workers, and seamstresses sewing soldiers' uniforms. A Southern woman named Catherine Edmondston wrote in her diary: "Ladies who never worked before are hard at work making uniforms and tents."[32] Another common war-related task assumed by women was service as "matrons of the regiment." Mostly soldiers' wives, they helped run army camps by acting as secretaries, laundresses, cooks, and nurses.

Those female nurses ended up playing crucial roles in the conflict because huge numbers of soldiers were wounded and required medical care. Working in both traditional hospitals and field hospitals (makeshift facilities set up near the battlefronts), more than three thousand Northern women served as nurses. Their superintendent was also a woman. Dorothea Dix earned great respect on both sides for advocating that captured Confederate fighters receive medical treatment comparable to that of Union ones.

Perhaps the best-known Civil War nurse was Clara Barton of Massachusetts (who in the postwar years went on to establish the American Red Cross). During one of the conflict's bloodiest battles, Antietam, in September 1862, she fearlessly brought a wagon filled with medical supplies and food right into the midst of the carnage. Bullets and shells flew around her for hours as she helped U.S. Army surgeon James Dunn tend to hundreds of badly wounded men. At one point a bullet whizzed through one of Barton's sleeves, but she ignored it and kept working. Astonished at her raw courage and dedication to duty, Dunn later famously called her "the true hero of the age, the angel of the battlefield."[33]

Still another way that women contributed to the war effort was by serving as spies. Rose O'Neal Greenhow, better known as Rebel Rose, for instance, secretly used her family connections to prominent Northerners to provide useful information to Confederate leaders. The Union had female spies, too. One was Elizabeth Van Lew, who brought baskets of food, medicine, and books to Union prisoners held in the Confederate capital, Richmond. While visiting,

Women Petition Congress to Abolish Slavery

Typical of the many antislavery petitions presented to Congress by women in the 1800s was this one drafted by a group of Massachusetts women.

The undersigned women of Massachusetts have been deeply convinced of the sinfulness of slavery and keenly aggrieved by its extension in a part of our country over which Congress possesses exclusive jurisdiction in all cases whatsoever, do most earnestly petition your honorable body immediately to abolish slavery in the District of Columbia, and to declare every human being free who sets foot on its soil. We also respectfully announce our intention to present this same petition, yearly, before your honorable body, that it may at least be "a memorial of us" that in the holy cause of human freedom, "we have done what we could."

Quoted in *London and Westminster Review*, July/April 1838, p. 10.

she quietly obtained data about enemy troop movements from the imprisoned Northern soldiers.

Another Crossroads

At war's end in 1865, American women once more found themselves at a crossroads. The organized fight for their rights had been resting on the back burner during the battle between North and South. Yet the work they had done during the war was so impressive that they had greatly enhanced their image in the eyes of men, including those in power. The most powerful of all, President Lincoln, remarked: "If all that has been said by orators and poets since the creation of the world were applied to the women of America, it would not do them justice for their conduct during this war."[34]

Thus, women facing the postwar years were more enthusiastic than ever about their chances for enhancing their social status. In the words of historian Harriet Sigerman, at war's end women's rights activists "forged ahead, ready to labor for their freedom. From their battles emerged many new ideas for achieving social and political equality for women."[35]

Chapter Three

The Long Road to the Ballot Box

By the close of the Civil War in 1865, many American men had more respect for women than they had before the war. During the conflict women on both sides had risen to the challenge and proved that they were patriotic, skilled in many areas, and extremely hardworking and dedicated. To the bitter disappointment of women's rights activists, however, most men did not yet see women as their equals. They were not ready even to consider extending voting rights to the female gender. Nor were most men prepared to give women equal pay for equal work. Also, in most cases in which women workers went on strike, they found their male bosses unwilling to give in to their demands for shorter hours and/or better working conditions. Despite all their hard work since the Seneca Falls Convention, therefore, Stanton, Mott, and other female rights activists were confronted with a sad truth. They faced many more years of struggle before they could either cast their ballots in elections or be treated as men's equals in the workplace.

Black Women's Double Handicap

Another dimension of that struggle involved race and the differing realities of life for white and black women. If the road toward voting rights and equality seemed long for white women, it appeared even longer for African American women. Thanks to the war, all black women were now free. However, the fact that they had long been enslaved and that their skin was dark put them in a more difficult position than that of white women. Most white Americans still viewed blacks as less intelligent, as well as morally inferior, to themselves.

That meant African American women had the double handicap of lesser status because they were women and because

An African American woman does laundry in the early 1900s. Despite gaining their freedom, most black women labored in jobs similar to those they had as slaves, often as domestics or field hands.

they were black. For the most part, the only work open to them was the same as when they were enslaved. Also, they received the lowest wages of any segment of the population.

In the immediate postwar years, therefore, most black women, especially in the South, did not see it as realistic to spend time demanding the right to vote and fighting for women's rights. They focused instead on seeing that their families survived and that their children had at least

a chance for a better life in the future. As an expert on women in this era explains:

Few freedwomen could indulge in full-time homemaking, because their families needed their economic contribution. Most black women did the same work in freedom that they had done in bondage—they worked in the fields or as midwives or domestic servants. Or they peddled poultry, eggs, fruit, and vegetables along the roads or at markets. But with freedom, something was different. To their way of thinking, they worked for their families, not for their employers, and these women organized their working life around family needs. Their sense of well-being was closely linked to their families' well-being. One mother, a cook, claimed that she could die happy, though she had spent much of her life in bondage, because her children would grow up in freedom.[36]

Amending the Constitution

Meanwhile, those women, white and black, who possessed the time and means to continue the struggle for women's rights came up against some unexpected obstacles. They had anticipated that after the war Congress would amend the Constitution to reflect the fact that slavery had been abolished. In their view, this presented a great opportunity to deal with women's lack of suffrage, or the right to vote. Hopefully lawmakers would word the new law so as to give both blacks and women that basic right.

Many women were sorely disappointed, however, when the Fourteenth Amendment, ratified in 1868, did not address their chief grievance. That law defined citizenship for African American men. Moreover, to the discontent of Stanton and other activists, it used the word "male" three times, which they felt seemed to question whether women were citizens at all. Stanton complained that the amendment created "an antagonism between black men and all women" that would allow men to continue dominating women, "especially in the southern states."[37]

Stanton and her colleagues were no less dissatisfied with the Fifteenth Amendment, ratified in 1870. It guaranteed the right to vote to all "citizens" regardless of race or color. Were women not citizens? the activists asked. Also, why had the lawmakers not included "sex" or "gender" along with race and color, which would have given women the vote? Various men in high positions were quick to answer these questions. One, a senator from Oregon, declared:

> The woman who undertakes to put her sex in an adversary position to man, who undertakes by the use of some independent political power [that is, voting] to contend and fight against man, displays a spirit which would, if able, convert all the now harmonious elements of society into a state of war, and make every home a hell on earth.[38]

Not surprisingly, the leaders of the women's movement were furious at such attempts to demean women and rationalize denying them suffrage. Stanton lashed out at such male attacks and the Fifteenth Amendment itself, saying:

> There is no true patriotism, no true nobility in tamely and silently submitting to this insult. [It] is licking

the hand that forges a new chain for our degradation. It is endorsing the old idea that woman's divinely ordained position is at man's feet, and not on an even platform by his side, [so that] the women of the Republic are now [expected] to touch the lowest depths of their political degradation.[39]

At this point it was clear to women's rights activists that their struggle to win suffrage was going to be long and difficult. The question was how they should go about achieving this goal. Some of them, including Stanton and Susan B. Anthony, condemned the Fifteenth Amendment. Stanton, who was angry that women had not gained the vote along with black men, began resorting to racial slurs. She even went so far as to suggest that only people who had attained a minimum educational level should be allowed to vote. This would have automatically disqualified many African Americans, both male and female, who as slaves had been denied schooling.

A number of women in the movement saw such views as unfair and too extreme. These self-identified moderates felt the better course was to endorse the Fifteenth Amendment and remain inclusive of all groups in the ongoing fight for women's rights. They decided to break away from those they labeled extremists. Largely under the leadership of activist Lucy Stone, in 1869 the moderates formed the American Woman Suffrage Association. That same year,

Stanton and Anthony established a rival organization, the National Woman's Suffrage Association, with Stanton as director. Although the members of these groups did not then foresee the consequences, this split in the women's movement proved counterproductive. It watered down its energies and impact and likely caused the struggle for female voting rights to go on longer than it would have if the activists had remained united.

Taking Advantage of Women Workers

In the meantime, a number of concerned women were fighting for better working conditions for members of their gender who worked in factories.

In the first few decades of the nineteenth century, the Industrial Revolution, which had begun in Britain in the previous century, began to take hold in the United States. Numerous factories were built, mostly in the northern states. At first, most of them, including the most successful in Lowell, Massachusetts, manufactured various kinds of textiles. By 1834, Lowell had nineteen textile mills that together produced some 27 million yards (24.7 million meters) of cotton cloth each year.

From that period through the end of the century, a major labor trend developed. Namely, the number of women workers in U.S. mills, other factories, and sweatshops (small-scale factories in which several people labored together in communal workrooms) continually increased. By 1860 sixty-two thousand

Women work in a Lowell textile mill in the 1850s. Factory jobs such as this meant low pay, long hours, and grueling conditions for the women who held them.

women worked in textile mills in New England alone.

In that same year, close to 30 percent of all workers in U.S. manufacturing were female, and by 1900 women made up the vast majority of those who toiled in sweatshops in cities.

One major reason that the owners of these businesses hired so many women was that, by long-standing custom, women made far less than men did in the same jobs. (For instance, in the early 1830s female printers in most northern cities made about fifty cents a day, whereas their male counterparts made three times that amount.) Hiring women therefore allowed factory owners to make higher profits.

Besides paying women low wages, these owners took advantage of them in other ways. Most female workers had few or no chances for advancement beyond the most menial positions, for example. Also, they often had to pay fines for making mistakes and endured unhealthy and/or dangerous working conditions. These included sixty-, seventy-, and even eighty-hour work weeks, inadequate lighting, poor ventilation, clothes or limbs getting caught

Women Belong in the Home?

Even after women had been working in factories for decades, some men felt they had no business working in jobs outside the home. A speaker at an 1866 meeting of a male labor organization explained this view:

Women's place is in the home, near her children. She should watch over them and instruct them in the first principles [of life]. From the physical, moral, and social point of view, women's [wage] labor must be vigorously condemned as the principal [cause] of the degradation [ruin] of the race. . . . Nature has endowed women with predetermined functions. Her place is in the family! [The] woman is the tie and the attraction that keeps the man at home, gives him habits of order and morality. . . . This is women's real work. It is a terrible mistake to impose another on her.

Quoted in Laura L. Frader, *The Industrial Revolution: A History in Documents*. New York: Oxford University Press, 2006, p. 129.

in machines, and fires and building collapses. (In January 1860 a textile mill in Lawrence, Massachusetts, collapsed, killing more than one hundred workers, mostly young women.)

As time went on, some courageous women stepped forward to try to reform the substandard conditions of their workplaces. One approach was to demand equal pay, or at least more than the poor wages most women received. But at a time when women still could not vote and had no say in politics or making laws, the concept of equal pay, or "comparable worth," was viewed as extremely radical. So requests for higher wages usually fell on deaf ears. (Women did not make major strides

toward comparable worth until the twentieth century.)

Reform Through Strikes and Disasters

Another approach to reform, one tried frequently by American women workers, was going on strike. The first known strike of female mill workers on their own (as opposed to women striking along with men) took place in Dover, New Hampshire, in 1828. Several hundred women astonished the community by walking out of the mill and staging a loud demonstration. They were protesting unfair new factory rules, including not allowing any talking on the job and imposing monetary fines on those late for work. Unfortunately for the women, nothing was gained. The owners made no concessions, fired the strike's organizers, and intimidated the others into returning to work by threatening to replace them with "better behaved women."[40]

The New Hampshire incident also set a precedent. Of the dozens of strikes launched by female workers in the nineteenth century, few achieved even moderate success. Not until a 1909 walkout of shirtwaist makers in New York City did American factory women win a major victory against their employers. (Around the turn of the century, a shirtwaist was a women's blouse tailored to look like a shirt.)

A somewhat more effective approach in the slow but steady movement to reform women's working conditions was the formation of unions. In the late 1800s and early 1900s, women's unions had little or no political clout. But they could help women help themselves through a variety of activities. A good example was the Women's Trade Union League (WTUL), established in 1903 by combining several smaller unions that represented female factory workers. The WTUL provided money, publicity, and other aid to smaller women's unions; supported individual strikes by women in industry in numerous cities; found meeting rooms where women could discuss their workplace grievances; helped women report labor law violations to the authorities; paid doctors to examine workers with health problems; and investigated working conditions in factories. After such investigations, the union informed the public about the substandard working conditions it had found. A pamphlet the WTUL published about adverse conditions in many textile mills said in part: "The weavers, the ring-spinners, the speeder-tenders, work in heat which is like the intense heat of the tropics, and at the end of the day's work [they] face the bitter cold nights of our northern winters. What a price we are paying for our cotton sheets and our calico."[41]

As time went on, the WTUL became even better organized and more effective. In 1907 its leaders adopted more challenging goals designed to aid working women, including, in their words, securing "for girls and women equal opportunity with boys and men in trades and technical training and pay on the basis of occupation and not on the basis of sex."[42] Also, in 1909 the union started lobbying legislators for an eight-hour workday and minimum wages for women. As a result, fourteen states adopted such wage laws between 1913 and 1923.

Despite the hard work and dedication of thousands of members of the women's labor movement, a considerable portion of workplace reforms were driven by public outrage over industrial disasters. The most notable example was the 1911 Triangle Shirtwaist Company fire. More than four hundred women labored in the company's ten-story building near Washington Square in New York City. On March 25 a fire, the cause of which remains unknown, started on the eighth floor. Those on

Firefighters try to stop a fire that destroyed the upper floors of the building of the Triangle Shirtwaist Company in 1911. The disaster, which killed 146 workers, mostly women, resulted in stronger workplace safety laws.

most of the floors managed to escape before the blaze spread; however, the employees on the ninth floor were not so fortunate. Unable to escape, many of them leaped from windows and fell to their deaths. A total of 146 workers, almost all women, perished in the disaster. The ensuing public uproar was so great that legislators in New York and other states hastily began creating stricter safety laws for factories and other workplaces.

Regaining Lost Momentum

By the time of the fire and the reforms it inspired, another major goal of the women's movement—suffrage—was finally making significant headway. By 1911 five states—Utah, Idaho, Washington, Wyoming, and Colorado—had already given women the right to vote. This trend of individual states approving female suffrage, despite the absence of a federal law allowing it, continued. In 1912 Arizona, California, Kansas, and

"They All Began to Drop"

On the day after the terrible Triangle Shirtwaist fire, an article on the front page of the New York Times *reported in part:*

At 4:40 o'clock [the] fire broke out. The one little fire escape in the interior was never resorted to by any of the doomed victims. Some of them escaped by running down the stairs, but in a moment or two this avenue was cut off by flame. The girls rushed to the windows and looked down at Greene Street, 100 feet below them. Then one poor, little creature jumped. There was a plate glass protection over part of the sidewalk, but she crashed through it, wrecking it and breaking her body into a thousand pieces. Then they all began to drop. The crowd yelled "Don't jump!" but it was jump or be burned, the proof of which is found in the fact that fifty burned bodies were taken from the ninth floor alone. . . . A heap of corpses lay on the sidewalk for more than an hour. The firemen were too busy dealing with the fire to pay any attention to people whom they supposed beyond their aid.

"141 Men and Girls Die in Waist Factory Fire; Trapped High Up in Washington Place Building; Street Strewn with Bodies; Piles of Dead Inside," *New York Times*, March 26, 1911, p. 1.

Oregon granted women the vote. Two years later, Nevada and Montana followed suit.

Meanwhile, the women's rights activists who had lost momentum in the 1870s managed to regain it. In 1890 the two organizations that had formed in 1869, splitting and weakening the movement, mended fences and agreed to merge. The new group was called the National American Woman Suffrage Association (NAWSA). It stepped up efforts to lobby congressmen to pass a constitutional amendment granting women's suffrage. Back in 1878 Susan B. Anthony had managed to get such an amendment introduced in Congress. It had not passed. But thereafter, bearing the unofficial title of the "Susan B. Anthony Amendment," it was reintroduced nearly every year.

Such efforts did not come without controversy. During these same years several anti–women's suffrage organizations formed. Their members, men and women alike, were convinced that giving women the right to vote posed serious threats to society. University of Kentucky scholar Kathleen M. Blee explains some of their worries:

Women's rights activist Inez Milholland rides a horse to lead a parade of thirty thousand suffragists in New York.

[They] maintained that extending the vote to women would reduce the special protections and routes of influence available to women, destroy the family, and increase the number of socialist-leaning voters. These sentiments dove-tailed with the fears of many Southern whites that female suffrage would undermine the [racist] Jim Crow restrictions that effectively [kept] African American voters in the South [from casting their ballots] and the apprehension of industrial and business leaders [that] women would vote in favor of social and political reform and for prohibiting the sale of liquor.[43]

Although such groups tried their best to discredit women suffragists, the latter forged ahead and continued to call attention to their grievances. One of the most audacious examples occurred in Washington, D.C., on March 3, 1913. Led by lawyer and female rights activist Inez Milholland, who proudly rode an imposing horse, more than five thousand women marched down Pennsylvania Avenue. Also in the parade were nine marching bands and about twenty-four colorful floats.

Another way that the suffragists gained attention, as well as credibility and new followers, was through their efforts to aid their country during World War I. The United States entered the conflict in April 1917. Immediately, American women rose to the challenge and volunteered to help in a wide variety of areas. Some twenty-thousand women, for example, crossed the ocean and worked as nurses near the battlefronts in France.

Back in the states, meanwhile, women grew victory gardens to provide food for the soldiers, organized war bond drives to raise money for the war effort, rolled bandages for the doctors and nurses, and worked in government relief agencies. Also, many thousands of women, taking the places of men who were off fighting, toiled in iron mills, munitions plants, and other factories. In fact, near the end of the war, women made up a whopping 20 percent of the country's industrial workforce, many of them maintaining homes and children at the same time. (At war's end, many of these women gave up the jobs to returning male veterans.) These combined efforts by American women to help win the war showed that as citizens they were no less patriotic, skilled, and worthy than American men. Many people who had long been opposed to allowing women to vote now changed their minds.

"A New and Good Thing"

In addition to their major wartime contributions, during the conflict, which ended in 1918, members of the women's movement continued their efforts to gain the vote. The leader of the NAWSA, Carrie Chapman Catt, coordinated various demonstrations and other peaceful protests with local suffrage groups across the nation. At the same time, a more radical splinter group, the National Women's Party (NWP), employed

Suffragists picket in front of the White House to draw attention to their cause in 1917. Although their protests were legal, many were arrested and jailed on false charges.

more militant means. Led by the daring Alice Paul of New Jersey, members of the NWP picketed the White House, then viewed by most Americans as an offensive, even hostile activity. When pressed to explain why she approved of such tactics, she replied: "If a creditor stands before a man's house all day long, demanding payment of his bill, the man must either remove the creditor or pay the bill."[44]

At first the authorities tolerated these protestors. But as time went on that attitude hardened, and a number of women were badly mistreated. According to researcher Deborah G. Felder:

Several months after the picketers started their silent White House vigil, the police began making arrests. The picketers, who had been demonstrating legally, were set free without sentence—at first. When they returned to the picket lines, they were arrested on a charge of obstructing sidewalk traffic, found guilty, and imprisoned in the Occaquan workhouse in Virginia. There Alice Paul, journalist Dorothy Day, and other picketers went on a hunger strike and were force-fed. Paul, whose hunger strike lasted twenty-two days, was considered insane by prison officials and forced to undergo a mental examination.[45]

These abuses culminated in what came to be known as the "Night of Terror." The male prison guards went on a rampage, beating and choking the women and leaving those they had injured in their cells with no medical treatment. When word of what had happened reached the public, there was widespread outrage. The courts pronounced most of the arrests invalid, and not long afterward the prisoners gained their freedom.

While the drama of the imprisoned NWP members was unfolding, the NAWSA stepped up its pressure on congressmen, urging them to pass the Anthony Amendment. Its members also lobbied the president, Woodrow Wilson, at every turn. Eventually he came around, agreed to back the bill, and began winning over legislators behind the scenes. As a result, on January 10,

The Night of Terror

This graphic depiction of the horrors encountered by some of the female picketers sent to a Virginia workhouse was penned by Pulitzer prize–winning columnist Connie Schultz.

The women were innocent and defenseless, but they were jailed nonetheless for picketing the White House, carrying signs asking for the vote. And by the end of the night, they were barely alive. Forty prison guards wielding clubs and their warden's blessing went on a rampage against the 33 women wrongly convicted of "obstructing sidewalk traffic." They beat Lucy Burns, chained her hands to the cell bars above her head, and left her hanging for the night, bleeding and gasping for air. They hurled Dora Lewis into a dark cell, smashed her head against an iron bed, and knocked her out cold. Her cellmate, Alice Cosu, thought Lewis was dead and suffered a heart attack. Additional [eyewitness accounts] describe the guards grabbing, dragging, beating, choking, slamming, pinching, twisting, and kicking the women. Thus unfolded the "Night of Terror" on Nov. 15, 1917, when the warden at the Occoquan Workhouse in Virginia ordered his guards to teach a lesson to the suffragists imprisoned there because they dared to picket Woodrow Wilson's White House for the right to vote.

Connie Schultz, "Our Debt to the Community Organizers Known as Suffragists," Create.com. www.creators.com/liberal/connie-schultz/our-debt-to-the-community-organizers-known-as-suffragists.html.

1918, after many years of rejecting the amendment, the House of Representatives passed it. The vote was 274 to 136, which achieved the two-thirds majority required to adopt a constitutional amendment.

All eyes now fell on the U.S. Senate, which also had to approve the bill for it to become law. There, to the suffragists' disappointment, the vote tally did not attain the needed two-thirds majority. Undaunted, the suffragists, still backed by the president, kept up their pressure on the senators, a strategy that worked. On June 4, 1919, the Senate voted again on the Anthony Amendment, which had

Alice Paul displays a banner from a balcony at the National Women's Party Headquarters to celebrate Tennessee's ratification of the Nineteenth Amendment in August 1920.

now come to be called the Nineteenth Amendment. This time the bill passed by a vote of 56 to 25.

In the next and final stage in the process, the legislation went to the states. Three-quarters of them had to ratify it for it to become law, a procedure that took a little more than a year. On August 24, 1920, the deciding state, Tennessee, mailed its certificate of ratification to Washington, D.C. When it arrived at the Capitol Building on August 26, the U.S. Secretary of State announced that the Nineteenth Amendment had offi-cially become part of the U.S. Constitution. Seventy-two years after a small meeting in upstate New York had set the women's movement in motion, a truly momentous victory had been achieved. At the NAWSA's Washington office, Carrie Chapman Catt told her staff: "It was a great crusade; the world has seen none more wonderful. . . . My admiration, love, and reverence go out to that band [of women who] fought and won a revolution, [with] congratulations that we were permitted to establish a new and good thing in the world."[46]

Chapter Four

Emergence of the New Public Woman

In the 1920s and 1930s, not long after women gained the right to vote, some of them took full advantage of their new political rights and ran for public office. Many lost their races, but a few were successful. Nellie Taylor Ross won the governorship of Wyoming in 1925, for instance. Also, in 1932 Hattie Caraway, a native of Arkansas, became the first woman elected to the U.S. Senate. Along with these high-profile political victories, a small number of women were elected to statewide and local offices in various sectors of the country.

In addition, some women with distinguished backgrounds and reputations achieved high public positions by appointment. Perhaps the best known example was Frances Perkins. When President Franklin D. Roosevelt (served 1933–1945) made her secretary of labor in 1933, she became the first woman to serve in a U.S. presidential cabinet. Roosevelt also appointed Marion Banister the first U.S. assistant treasurer and Ruth Bryan Owen the first woman ambassador to a foreign nation (Denmark).

Yet despite these accomplishments, the vast majority of office-holders in the nation were still men. Indeed, during the post–World War I era, women in the political arena remained few in number. Moreover, on the whole they wielded very little power.

By contrast, the social strides made by women in the same period were more numerous and certainly more visible. Between the passage of the Nineteenth Amendment in 1920 and the end of World War II in 1945, what some experts have described as a new public woman emerged in the American social sphere. Though only marginally more politically advanced than her mother, she was far more open to enjoying popular activities that women of the preceding generation had viewed as unacceptable, even shocking. Among others, these included drinking alcohol, dancing in public, attending nightclubs, swearing, and wearing makeup on a regular basis. In short, the new woman wanted to be able to express herself as openly as men had been doing for generations. As scholar Sarah J. Deutsch explains, many women

believed the most important thing to leave behind was "sex-consciousness," their sense of themselves as women who shared interests with other women. [They] opted instead for individualism. "Breaking into the human race," as they put it, and individual success in the world . . . became their goals. [For] them, individuality became a way to allow for diversity among women, and [in the 1920s, 1930s, and 1940s] it would lead to models of individual accomplishment.[47]

Another Change in Womanhood?

The new female social image that first emerged in the 1920s was most represented by the so-called flapper. (The term was coined by screenwriter Frances Marion in the 1920 silent film *The Flapper*.) With a few exceptions she was a young, fun-loving, and carefree woman. Flappers also typically thought their parents and other elders were too serious about life, even boring. In the words of historian Sara Evans:

[Flappers] wanted to have fun. Newspapers, magazines, movies, and novels all told Americans that womanhood had changed again. Young, [and] hedonistic [pleasure seeking], the flapper soon became a symbol of the age, with her bobbed hair, powdered nose, rouged cheeks, and shorter skirts. Lively and energetic, she wanted experience for its own sake. She sought out popular amusements in cabarets, dance halls, and movie theaters that no respectable, middle-class woman would have frequented a generation before. She danced, smoked, and flaunted her sexuality to the horror of her elders.[48]

The lighthearted, cheerful flapper image mirrored the generally positive outlook of the times. The 1920s in the United States, Britain, and a few other developed countries was characterized by widespread prosperity and optimism. This was reflected in some of the nicknames for the era, such as the "Roaring Twenties" and the "Jazz Age." Cities were rapidly expanding, and they featured a wide array of entertaining pastimes, many of them new or relatively so, including nightclubs, movies, radio, jazz concerts, modern art, and dance marathons. Many women wanted, and indeed demanded, to enjoy these and other leisure pursuits along with men.

It would be misleading, however, to suggest that all women were flappers, carefree, or even happy during that decade. Such fortunate women were

Flappers dance at a nightclub in 1926. Flappers' fashions and fun-loving lifestyles reflected women's changing social image in the 1920s.

usually white and members of the middle and upper classes. A few supported themselves. But more commonly they came from families in which their husbands or fathers had well-paying jobs. So such women had ample money to shop, party, and otherwise enjoy the age's expanding consumer and fun-oriented culture.

In stark comparison, most poor and minority women, of which there were many, remained in the same underprivileged socioeconomic situations they had been in for decades. These women continued to endure regular hardship, hunger, worry, and stress. Evans writes:

> Salesgirls found it difficult to maintain the required [friendly smiles] as they sold wealthy women goods that they themselves could never afford to buy. Racist hiring poli-

cies prevented many black women . . . from experiencing the economic fruits of an expanding service sector. [They] found themselves forced into a very narrow range of job opportunities—the least desirable factory jobs and domestic service [maids, cooks, and so forth].[49]

The Fight for Rights in Decline

Whether a woman in the Roaring Twenties was well-off or poor, or able to enjoy her life or not, she still had certain rights that the women of her mother's generation had fought hard to acquire. Chief among these was the right to vote. Many of the former suffragists and other activists were content with this level of progress and felt that their work was largely done. Reflecting that attitude, in 1920 the NAWSA changed its name to the League of Women Voters. The new organization's main goal was not to win more rights for women but rather to train young women to become good citizens.

The smaller and more radical NWP, still led by Alice Paul, was less satisfied, however. Paul and her colleagues felt that gaining the vote had been an important step but that women were still far from equal and must continue to assert themselves. In 1922 spokeswomen for the organization stated their goal:

To remove the discriminations against women in the laws of the United States is the beginning of [our] determined effort to secure the freedom of women, an integral part of the struggle for human liberty for which women are first of all responsible. [Our] interest lies in the final release of woman from the class of a dependent, subservient being to which early civilization committed her.[50]

The chief tool the NWP chose to attain the goal of full equality was another constitutional amendment, which became known as the Equal Rights Amendment (ERA). Written by Paul herself, it stated rather simply that men and women should have equal rights in all U.S. states and territories. The use of the broad term "rights," as opposed to naming specific rights, was intended to be umbrella-like and cover all rights, including legal ones. Opponents feared, quite rightly, that giving women legal equality with men would force employers to provide equal pay for women and end other forms of discrimination against women. Despite widespread opposition, the NWP persevered and in 1923 managed to secure a congressional hearing on the amendment. But it had no chance of becoming law. At the time, no one realized that it would be several decades before Congress saw fit to pass it.

Partly because the ERA was rejected in the 1920s, the struggle for expanded rights in the women's movement declined in that decade. Another reason was that the U.S. War Department

VOTE

BALLOT BOX

Bonhajo

League of Women Voters

The Equal Rights Amendment

The original draft of the Equal Rights Amendment, or ERA, was written by noted suffragist Alice Paul in 1921, shortly after the ratification of the Nineteenth Amendment. She introduced the new document to her colleagues at a 1923 commemoration of the 1848 Seneca Falls Convention. Then informally called the "Lucretia Mott Amendment," its core sentiment stated: "Men and women shall have equal rights throughout the United States and every place subject to its jurisdiction." This wording was later changed somewhat, and the version of the bill that eventually passed Congress reads as follows:

> Section 1. Equality of rights under the law shall not be denied or abridged by the United States or by any state on account of sex.
>
> Section 2. The Congress shall have the power to enforce, by appropriate legislation, the provisions of this article.
>
> Section 3. This amendment shall take effect two years after the date of ratification.

"The History Behind the Equal Rights Amendment," Alice Paul Institute. www.equalrightsamendment .org/era.htm.

suspected, wrongly it turned out, that many women's organizations were pacifistic and had ties to communism. That dissuaded numerous women from joining these groups. In addition, women's unions virtually disappeared, making it more difficult for female workers to fight inequality in the workplace.

In the years directly following the passage of the Nineteenth Amendment,

A poster from the League of Women Voters, formerly known as the National American Woman Suffrage Association, urges women to use their newly acquired right to vote in the 1920s.

therefore, women made little headway in political, legal, or labor rights. The only significant improvement in their status was their increased acceptance by most men in various social and public spheres and situations, which did prove to be a major and permanent advancement for the female gender.

The Depression and Poor Women

Had the economic prosperity of the 1920s continued into the 1930s, women may have managed to translate their improved social standing into increased upper mobility (better jobs, pay, and influence). In turn, that might have led to some substantial political and legal gains. However, the 1930s witnessed the sudden spread of considerable *downward* mobility for most women, and for many men as well.

This unexpected reversal of fortune was caused by the onset of the Great Depression. The initial spark for this decade-long period of severe economic losses and increased poverty and misery was the crash of the U.S. Stock Exchange in October 1929. In the first month alone, investors lost more than $50 billion, equivalent to many hundreds of billions of dollars today.

As a result of this tremendous financial disaster, the entire U.S. economy went into a fatal tailspin. Like a collapsing house of cards, as one sector of the economy fell, it took another with it, which took down still another. Hundreds of banks failed, causing millions of people to lose most or all of their money. Barely able to make ends meet, if they could at all, they started purchasing only the barest necessities. That seriously hurt stores, factories, and other businesses, large and small, which either downsized or went out of business by the tens of thousands, throwing millions of people out of work. By the early months of 1930, the U.S. unemployment rate, which had been 3 percent before the great crash, had risen to 9 percent; it was a dismal 16 percent in 1931 and a crippling 25 percent in early 1933.

The manner in which the economic catastrophe affected women depended in large degree on their, or their fami-

An unemployed woman sells apples on a New York City street during the Great Depression.

lies', financial positions. The handful of rich women whose families did not lose their fortunes in the crash retained their wealth and influence. The rest, making up more than 99 percent of the female population, were roughly divided into two groups—poor, often destitute women, and middle-class women.

The plight of poor women and their families was often horrendous. Huge numbers of such families were homeless. Many became migrants who moved regularly from one town or state to another looking for whatever temporary jobs they could find. Usually they lived in tents or makeshift shelters in fields or wooded areas. Also, large numbers of poor women did not have enough to eat much of the time and suffered from a range of health problems as a result. It was common to see women selling apples on street corners or lining up each day, sometimes for hours, to get loaves of bread provided by charities. One charity worker later remembered a desperate woman who "went along the docks and picked up vegetables that fell from the wagons. Sometimes the fish vendors gave her fish at the end of the day. On two different occasions, the family was without food for a day and a half."[51]

The situation was dire for the majority of American women, but because of ingrained societal racism, especially in the South, the situation for African

Forced into Less Desirable Jobs

The lack of good jobs open to women during the Great Depression, often resulting in their downward social mobility, is well stated by San Jose State University scholar Lois Rita Helmbold.

Female employees in restaurants, hotels, [and] laundries . . . suffered enormous joblessness, because consumers could not afford these services. Women industrial workers also sustained high unemployment. If they lost their jobs, women scrambled to stay employed and moved down the ladder of desirable occupations in order to find work. Elementary school teachers became secretaries, secretaries took jobs as waitresses, waitresses moved into laundries, and laundry [workers] became domestic [servants]. Some wives and mothers sought jobs for the first time, and women of every occupational background took domestic jobs. Fewer jobs, increased competition, and downward mobility ensured that young, white, single, attractive, Christian women had the best opportunities for employment, while older, black women were the most likely to be pushed out of the work force.

Lois Rita Helmbold, "Great Depression," in *The Reader's Companion to U.S. Women's History*, eds. Wilma Mankiller et al. Boston: Houghton Mifflin, 1998, pp. 245–46.

American women was often worse. First, in the early to mid-1930s the unemployment rate for blacks was at least 50 percent. Many African American women could not find any sort of work. Moreover, those who did have jobs—most often as field hands, laundresses, and maids—were paid a fraction of what white women made for the same work.

Scrimping to Make Ends Meet

Of the millions of women considered middle class during the Depression, a few held part-time or full-time jobs. Others frequently looked for work but could not find it. Both of these groups were affected by gender bias. Some misguided people believed that working women took jobs away from men, who were thereby unemployed and unable to support their families. Because of such discrimination, in the mid- to late 1930s, 63 percent of public utility companies, 65 percent of banks, and 84 percent of insurance companies refused to hire women. Well-known journalist Norman Cousins ignorantly boasted that he had a quick fix for the ailing economy. "Simply fire the women," he quipped, "who shouldn't be working anyway, and hire the men. Presto! No unemployment. No relief rolls. No Depression."[52]

A majority of middle-class women did make men like Cousins happy by remaining stay-at-home housewives. They did their best to scrimp and downsize to make ends meet so that they and their families could continue to have a roof over their heads. According to one expert:

The typical woman during the Depression years had a husband who was still working, although he had probably taken a pay cut in order to keep his job. These wives, always budget conscious, now struggled to make do with less. They practiced such economies as buying day-old bread, warming several dishes in the oven at the same time to save gas, buying cheaper cuts of meat, and substituting cheap ingredients in some recipes. They sewed blankets into coats, and cut down adult clothes to fit children. Families moved to smaller houses or to apartments and cut out or cut down on luxuries and entertainments such as movies and Sunday drives. Instead they stayed home and listened to the radio.[53]

Strong Female Role Models

These middle-class women, along with most other Americans of their gender, looked up to a small group of elite women who broke new ground during the Depression. Most of these female role models were middle-aged or older. Several had earlier worked as suffragists and knew how to organize and work toward solving problems and other goals. It was from their ranks that President Roosevelt chose women like Frances Perkins to help create new government policies to deal with the economic crisis. Perkins became instrumental in fashioning the Social Security program, for example. It provided badly needed aid to needy older women and men from 1935 on and remains a bedrock of the government safety net for elderly Americans today.

Another of Roosevelt's capable female appointees, Mary McLeod Bethune, ran the Office of Minority Affairs for the National Youth Administration. She also had the distinction of being the first African American to head a U.S. government agency. Bethune was a highly intelligent, hardworking, and determined individual. She proved that even in the face of entrenched racism and sexism, a woman of her talents could rise to a position of influence in a country that was slowly but steadily shedding its long-standing biases against females.

The most widely known and respected woman in Depression-era America was Roosevelt's wife, First Lady Eleanor Roosevelt. A strong supporter of women's causes, she urged her husband to utilize the talents of as many women as possible. She also made sure that women who had workable ideas for government programs were granted access to the White House and members of the president's cabinet. In addition,

President Franklin D. Roosevelt appointed educator and activist Mary McLeod Bethune to run the Office of Minority Affairs for the National Youth Administration, making her the first African American to head a U.S. government agency.

she allowed only female reporters to cover her own news conferences. This forced every news outlet that desired to cover the White House to hire at least one woman. In turn, a number of other young women were inspired to seek college educations and careers in journalism. Thus, although there was little in the way of organized female rights activism in the 1930s, some members of the next generation of women were learning to better themselves by example.

Women in World War II

As the 1930s gave way to the next decade, many American women suddenly found themselves with unexpected opportunities to work and contribute to society in new ways. The United States entered World War II the day after Japanese planes bombed the American military bases on Hawaii's island of Oahu on December 7, 1941. Millions of American men quickly enlisted, creating an enormous labor shortage. To fill their places, large numbers of women, eventually surpassing 18 million, rose to the challenge. Of these, about 3 million worked in factories making war-related and other materials. The rest labored in more customarily female occupations, such as waitress and secretary.

The women who took jobs in factories, many of which made guns, airplanes, tanks, jeeps, and other war machines, were particularly important to the war effort. Both to attract women to such jobs and to celebrate their patriotism and capabilities, the government

Women of the U.S. Women's Army Auxiliary Corps travel by military vehicle to their assignment in North Africa in 1942.

Rosie Says "We Can Do It!"

The chief visual image of "Rosie the Riveter," the fictional character who became a symbol of American female industrial workers during the war, was a painting by artist J. Howard Miller. It showed a white woman with brown hair rolling up her sleeve (an action representing getting down to work) and simultaneously flexing her right bicep, a typically male gesture. The image was part of a series of posters commissioned by Westinghouse Company and created by Miller to support the war effort. Another famous image of "Rosie" was illustrated by renowned artist Norman Rockwell for the cover of the *Saturday Evening Post* in May 1943. As part of a propaganda effort, government officials located other "Rosies" across the country—women who were photographed in poses mimicking the one in the paintings—and employed them in various media ads.

The image of Rosie the Riveter became an iconic symbol of women's contributions to the war effort during World War II.

sponsored propaganda campaigns. The most famous featured the tough, proud fictional character Rosie the Riveter. Artist J. Howard Miller produced the iconic image of her seen on millions of posters and in other ads.

Also, some 350,000 women served in the military during the war. Some were WACS (Women's Army Corps), a part of the U.S. Army established in 1942. Others joined the WAVES (Navy), SPARS (Coast Guard), WASPs (Air Force), or other similar groups. These military women performed a wide range of jobs. Among others, they included mechanic, electrician, radio operator, secretary, weather observer and forecaster, cryptographer (code breaker), sheet metal worker, parachute rigger, aerial photograph analyst, control tower operator, and file clerk. In addition, nearly eighty thousand American women served as nurses in the conflict.

Unfortunately for African American women, and the country, they were sorely underutilized in the war, primarily because of overt racism, which was still rampant in American society. They were excluded altogether from serving in the WASPs. Other service branches did accept a few black women, but they were segregated from white women. This did not prevent them from disproving their supposed inferiority by serving with distinction.

Indeed, the outstanding performance of females of all colors in both industry and the military during the war became an important factor in changing social attitudes about women. In turn, that led to their increased acceptance in the workplace in the postwar years. In fact, many historians credit women's wide-ranging work experiences between 1941 and 1945 with partially motivating a revival of the women's movement in the 1960s.

Chapter Five

Rising Demands for Gender Equality

W orld War II had given millions of American women the chance to work outside the home, many of them for the first time. But these opportunities did not become an automatic springboard for the female gender's continued social advancement after the conflict. Instead, society's postwar expectations for women seemed to revert to the prewar and traditional notion that they primarily belonged in the home. According to University of Minnesota scholar Elaine T. May:

Although the vast majority of women who worked [during] the war wanted to keep their jobs, many lost their wartime positions to the returning [male] veterans. Men and women alike were expected to [give up] their emergency roles and settle into domestic life— men as breadwinners, women as homemakers. In this vision, there

was no room for the independent single woman, nor the married career woman. After the war, all major institutions in which Americans lived and worked came to foster the vision of a nation finding its ultimate security in the traditional American home.[54]

A crucial element of that tradition of the secure American home was having babies. Indeed, after the war both men and women were eager to start families, and this appeared more financially viable than it had been since the prosperous years of the 1920s. The postwar American economy was booming, and most men had jobs. So Americans perceived no pressing need for most women to work. They could concentrate on having babies instead, and they did so, producing the famous baby boom, in which the birthrate in America skyrocketed. "The Baby Boom," May says, "was a statistical indicator of the intense focus on family life that permeated the nation in the years after World War II."[55]

The period from 1945 to the mid-1960s was therefore one in which many Americans settled into social roles that were more or less expected of them. Large numbers aspired to what came to be seen as the social ideal. It centered on the comfortable, middle-class, all-white, and decidedly strife-free home life

A family sings together in their living room. This portrayal shows the happy middle-class domestic life that became the social ideal in 1950s America.

dramatized in such 1950s TV shows as *Leave It to Beaver*. That model for American life was just that—ideal. It ignored several existing social problems, including poverty, racism against blacks, and sexism against women. These brewed beneath the surface, so to speak, until they burst forth into the public sphere in the 1960s. As a result, from then until the early 1980s, women's rights activism returned to American life with an intensity not seen since the days of the suffragists.

Women's "Homemaker" Image Outdated?

The new struggle for women's rights, sometimes called the second wave of feminism (the first wave being the fight for suffrage), was not the first social ill the country dealt with in the 1960s. That distinction fell to the civil rights movement, in which African Americans fought for equal treatment and respect. Major civil rights legislation passed by Congress in 1964 and 1965 was not able to create instant equality. Nor could it make up for all the wrongs blacks had suffered for generations. However, the new laws did put African Americans on the road to social acceptance and equal treatment under the law.

That second goal, equal treatment under the law, was, and indeed always had been, the chief objective of the women's movement as well. So blacks' ongoing fight for civil rights inspired many women to become active, as their grandmothers had been, in seeking their own equality. These women felt that the "homemaker" image of American women so prevalent in the 1950s was outdated and unfair. They argued that large numbers of women either had to work to support themselves and their families or desired to have their own careers in addition to or instead of their role as housewives.

For these reasons, they said, the proportion of females in the workplace was growing. Statistics bore this out. In 1940, 15 percent of American women worked outside the home; by 1950 it was 25 percent; and by 1960 it was 39 percent. Also by 1960, 10 million American families featured wives holding down full- or part-time jobs in addition to their husbands' full-time occupations. These facts reflected certain social trends of the prior four to five decades, aptly summarized by historian Sara Evans:

Women lived longer and had fewer children—despite the [short-term] Baby Boom, the long-term trends remained clear. They also married younger and concentrated their childbearing in the early years of marriage. Together, these changes resulted in a new post-child-rearing life stage, relatively free of child care responsibilities. Most women worked in urban areas, the location of most new jobs. [Because of] increased educational opportunities . . . young women were likely to move straight from school to marriage expecting to work until they had children and possibly again when the children were older.[56]

The idealized image of the American homemaker during the 1950s did not reflect the reality of many women of that era who sought further opportunities in jobs, education, and social standing.

In short, the idea of women pursuing jobs or careers at will, in the same way that men did, was becoming the norm. Yet a certain social stigma against such female independence still remained. What is more, women still did not receive equal treatment in the workplace, demonstrated by the reality that they earned considerably less than men for perform- ing the same jobs. Many women felt that it was only fair that society address such gender-related inequities.

"To Take Action" for Women

These rising grievances motivated a few influential women, notably Assistant Secretary of Labor Esther Peterson,

Educate Her to Her Full Potential

The following excerpt from the National Organization for Women's statement of purpose, drafted in 1966, calls for allowing women to become as well educated as the best-educated men.

We believe that it is as essential for every girl to be educated to her full potential of human ability as it is for every boy—with the knowledge that such education is the key to effective participation in today's economy and that, for a girl as for a boy, education can only be serious where there is expectation that it will be used in society. . . . We consider the decline in the proportion of women receiving higher and professional education to be evidence of discrimination. This discrimination may take the form of quotas against the admission of women to colleges and professional schools; lack of encouragement by parents, counselors, and educators; [or] denial of loans or fellowships. [We] believe that the same serious attention must be given to high school dropouts who are girls as to boys.

Quoted in Betty Friedan, *It Changed My Life: Writings on the Women's Movement*. New York: Random House, 1976, p. 89.

to approach President John F. Kennedy shortly after he took office in 1961. They urged him to establish what became known as the Presidential Commission on the Status of Women. He did so that year, asking the group's members to determine where women stood in society and to suggest ways in which their situation might be improved.

The commission issued its report, titled "The American Woman," in 1963. It detailed serious antifemale discrimination in employment, including unequal pay; lack of child care and other social services; inequality in education; and various forms of legal inequality. On the basis of these findings, the president immediately ordered two impor- tant reforms. First, he required that hiring for all civil service, or government, jobs, must be done "solely on the basis of ability to meet the requirements of the position, and without regard to sex [that is, gender]."[57]

Kennedy also pushed the Equal Pay Act (EPA) through Congress. The new law banned employers from paying women less than men for the same work. Although the EPA was spottily enforced and did not eradicate unequal pay practices, overall its effect was positive. When it passed in 1963, women made about fifty-nine cents for each dollar a man made for the same job. By 1970 that ratio had risen to sixty-two cents per dollar.

Although Kennedy's reforms were helpful, concerned women felt that many more reforms were needed. For that to happen, American women needed to be well-informed about the problems the gender faced. They also needed to learn to organize and lobby for new reforms in the same way the suffragists had in the century's early decades. To these ends, in the same year the EPA passed, noted writer and activist Betty Friedan published her book *The Feminine Mystique*. It detailed how women had been largely relegated to the home in the years following World War II and called attention to the many social inequalities women were still forced to deal with.

In addition, in 1966 Friedan established the National Organization for Women (NOW). It provided American women with a group that could fight for their rights through the media, the courts, and Congress. NOW's initial statement of intent began, "The purpose of NOW is to take action to bring women into full participation in the

A woman makes a public call for pay equity for women in the early 1970s. Despite the signing of the Equal Pay Act in 1963, women still struggle in many occupations to make equal pay.

Lies About Welfare Mothers

Among the many women's organizations that formed in the 1960s and 1970s was the National Welfare Rights Organization. Its goal was to convince lawmakers and the public that, despite much bad press aimed at the poor women who received welfare, a majority of them badly needed it to survive. One member of the organization stated in 1972:

People still believe that old lie that [welfare] mothers keep having kids just to get a bigger welfare check. On the average, another baby means another $35 a month—barely enough for food and clothing. Having babies for profit is a lie that only men could make up, and only men could believe. Men, who never had to bear the babies or have to raise them. . . . There are a lot of other lies that male society tells about welfare mothers; that [they] are immoral, that [they] are lazy, misuse their welfare checks, spend it all on booze and are stupid and incompetent. If people are willing to believe these lies, it's partly because they're just special versions of the lies society tells about *all* women.

Quoted in *Liberation News Service*, vol. 415, February 26, 1972, pp. 15–16.

mainstream of American society now, exercising all the privileges and responsibilities thereof in truly equal partnership with men."[58] In some ways NOW was a modern version of the 1848 Seneca Falls Convention, that is, a platform to support a women's rights movement. NOW members pushed for passage of the Equal Rights Amendment (ERA) and abortion rights, urged strong enforcement of existing federal laws against discrimination, and organized public protests against gender discrimination.

Thanks to these and other organized activities designed to further women's equality, NOW and other similar organizations rapidly gained new members. The growing new women's movement did not reach or inspire every female American, but those it did reach felt their lives were changed for the better. In 1967 a recent Harvard University graduate named Sara Ruddick wrote in her diary that the women's movement

enabled me to achieve a new self-respect at home, made me confident and clear about my need for the friendship of women. [Before] I had carried an invisible, almost amorphous [shapeless] weight, the weight of guilt and apology for [having] interests and ambitions that should have been a source of pride [but that some men said women should not be doing]. When that weight was lifted, I felt almost literally lighter, certainly more energetic, more concentrated.[59]

Walls Begin to Crack

By 1970 the main thrust of the new women's movement was popularly known by the shorthand term "women's lib" (short for "liberation"). Women who had the time and energy did their part for the cause by taking part in marches, writing or calling their congressperson, and making monetary contributions to women's organizations. Among average, nonactivist women, meanwhile, some were big supporters of the movement and were pleased when they heard about strides made by organizations like NOW.

Other women, however, disapproved of the entire women's movement and everything it stood for. Conservative lawyer and writer Phyllis Schlafly called feminists "a bunch of bitter women seeking a constitutional cure for their personal problems."[60] She went on to say:

> They view the home as a prison, and the wife and mother as a slave. [Women's lib] is a total assault on the role of the American woman as wife and mother, and on the family as the basic unit of society.... They are promoting "day-care centers" for babies instead of homes. They are promoting abortions instead of families.[61]

Whether one agreed or disagreed with the women's movement and its activism, no one doubted that it was having a growing effect on society. The front page of a January 1970 issue of the *New York Times* pointed out: "The walls of economic and psychological discrimination against women in the American job market are beginning to crack under the pressures of the Federal Government, the women's liberation movement, and the efforts of thousands of individual women themselves."[62]

The walls of discrimination the article referred to cracked further as 1970 progressed. Women made increasingly bold statements, both in writing and in public. On March 18 two hundred women staged a sit-in at the New York City offices of the *Ladies' Home Journal* and for eleven hours engaged its editor John Mack Carter and his assistants in fervent debate. A magazine that claimed to support women, the protestors said, should pay its female employees a living wage. It should also provide day care for its employees and hire more minorities. Carter listened intently and agreed to publish an eight-page account of the event and the demonstrators' demands in that year's August issue. He stated in the account:

> Beneath the shrill accusations and the radical dialectic [argument], our editors heard some convincing truths about the persistence of sexual discrimination in many areas of American life. [We] seemed to catch a rising note of angry self-expression among today's American women, a desire for representation, for recognition, for a broadening range of alternatives [in their lives].[63]

The supportive statements Carter made about women's lib resonated with special force because the August issue in which they appeared coincided with the fiftieth anniversary of the passage of the Nineteenth Amendment in 1920. To hammer the message home even harder, a few days later, on August 26, NOW sponsored a so-called Women's Strike for Equality. Tens of thousands of women marched and protested in cities and towns across the nation. These demonstrations were so effective that in the weeks and months that followed, the membership of NOW chapters in all corners of the country swelled. Meanwhile, feminists from NOW and other women's organizations stepped up their lobbying and educational efforts. They wrote books and magazine articles, went on TV and radio talk shows, and lectured at colleges and local community gatherings.

A Golden Touch?

The visibility and influence of the women's movement expanded as it never had before. In the ensuing two years, a series of dramatic events propelled women's rights issues into the forefront of American life, conversation, debate, and legislative and legal decisions. In 1971, for instance, Betty Friedan, Congresswomen Bella Abzug and Shirley Chisholm, jour-

Women demonstrate in favor of equal rights in Washington, D.C., in August 1970. This demonstration coincided with the NOW-sponsored Women's Strike for Equality to mark the fiftieth anniversary of the passage of the Nineteenth Amendment.

nalist Gloria Steinem, and several other leading feminists established the National Women's Political Caucus (NWPC). It was a bipartisan organization, meaning that it was open to members of both major political parties. One goal of the NWPC was to recruit and train feminist-minded women for government offices. Another was to help them get elected or appointed to those offices. The officeholders themselves then proceeded to lobby hard for various social and political objectives, including better education for women, legislation banning discrimination against women, and passage of the ERA.

Gloria Steinem was instrumental in creating another powerful tool to advance women's causes in that same year. She became the publisher and editor of a new magazine called *Ms.* This term had been recently coined by feminists to replace Miss and Mrs., which indicate marital status. Since men were addressed by just one term—Mr.—which does *not* reveal said status, feminists felt that, in fairness, women should also be addressed by an equally nonjudgmental term. The first national feminist magazine, *Ms.* carried articles dealing with women's issues, among them abortion rights, domestic violence, equality in the workplace, and many more. The magazine, which premiered in January 1972, was an instant and huge success. The first three hundred thousand copies sold out in just eight days.

The early 1970s also witnessed a flurry of national legislation designed to ensure more gender equality in the country. In 1972 Congress passed and President Richard M. Nixon signed into law the Equal Employment Opportunity Act. Among other things, it created the Equal Employment Opportunity Commission (EEOC). The EEOC investigates claims submitted to it that some sort of discrimination has occurred in the workplace. If the agency determines reasonable cause for the claim, it can sue the employer in a federal court.

Nixon also signed an educational bill best known as Title IX. It bans discrimination in all educational institutions that receive federal money. Many such schools had earlier maintained limits on the number of women they accepted in certain programs. The effect of the new law, which eliminated these limits, was dramatic. In 1972, 9 percent of medical degrees in the country were earned by women, compared to 38 percent in 1994. Experts credited much of the increase to Title IX. The law also requires that schools receiving federal funds offer women equal opportunities to play sports as those offered men.

Also in 1972, under intense lobbying by women's groups, Congress finally passed the Equal Rights Amendment. This was seen as a major victory, especially considering that the bill's opponents had lobbied just as hard to stop it. Phyllis Schlafly had claimed that if the ERA passed, women would lose the right to child support and alimony during a divorce, be drafted by the military, and go into combat. She claimed that the ERA went against God, who had created females to have babies and take care of

their families. "It's simply the way God made us,"[64] she said. In the end, lawmakers did not buy these arguments, and on March 22 the amendment went to the states for ratification.

Still another event that feminists viewed as a victory occurred in 1973. In a case known as *Roe v. Wade*, the U.S. Supreme Court ruled that a woman could not be denied the right to an abortion performed during the first trimester of pregnancy. The decision was and still is viewed as highly controversial. Yet at the time, it seemed to cap the stunning series of pro-women developments of the previous two years. Many feminists felt as if they had, in one historian's words, "a golden touch."[65]

Positive Change Will Continue

No winning streak lasts forever, however, as was illustrated by the eventual fate of the ERA. After its passage by Congress in 1972, the bill made its way through the state legislatures for close to ten years.

But when the deadline for ratification came in 1982, it remained three states short of the thirty-eight required to make it the law of the land. Part of the reason that some state legislatures rejected the bill was that women tended to see it as more important than men did. In the three pivotal states, for example, 75 percent of the female legislators voted for the ERA, whereas only 46 percent of the men did so. Continued denunciations of the amendment by Phyllis Schlafly and other opponents also hurt its ratification.

In addition, some state-level politicians worried that the ERA would give too much power to the federal government at the states' expense.

The demise of the ERA, at least for the time being, was a serious blow to American feminists. By the early 1980s they were also disappointed that the laws against discrimination passed in the previous two decades had not brought about change fast enough. Some in the woman's movement, however, pointed out that

Phyllis Schlafly, an outspoken opponent of the Equal Rights Amendment, campaigned against its ratification in the 1970s and 1980s.

A Woman Opposed to Women's Lib

Conservative writer and activist Phyllis Schlafly came out strongly against the Equal Rights Amendment during the 1970s. In the following statement, made in February 1972, she argues that the women's movement is unnecessary because American women are not oppressed.

In the last couple of years, a noisy movement has sprung up agitating for "women's rights." Suddenly, everywhere we are afflicted with aggressive females on television talk shows yapping about how mistreated American women are, suggesting that marriage has put us in some kind of "slavery," that housework is menial and degrading, and—perish the thought—that women are discriminated against. . . . It's time to set the record straight. The claim that American women are downtrodden and unfairly treated is the fraud of the century. The truth is that American women never had it so good. . . . The "women's lib" movement is *not* an honest effort to secure better jobs for women who want or need work outside the home. [Instead, it] is a total assault on the role of the American woman as wife and mother, and on the family as the basic unit of society.

Quoted in Nancy MacLean, ed., *The American Women's Movement, 1945–2000*. New York: St. Martin's, 2009, pp. 116–17.

new laws, especially those that challenge entrenched social views and behaviors, take decades to make a difference. On the positive side, these optimists pointed out, women had found new roles and greater respect in the workplace. They had also gained a greater voice in government, expanded educational opportunities, and the right to decide for themselves whether a pregnancy should or should not be terminated. Overall, they added, feminist concerns and organizations were now a regular and permanent part of the American social and political scene. This would ensure that positive change would continue in the future, even if slowly.

Chapter Six

A Continuing Fight for Status and Rights

In the wake of the failure of the states to ratify the ERA in 1982, American women entered a new phase of their social and political advancement, one that is still ongoing. In the 1980s, 1990s, and beyond, NOW and other women's organizations continued to work hard for women's causes. Also, a number of advances for women occurred in politics, the workplace, the military, and other areas. Indeed, so many advances took place that those who were young women in the 1970s are often astonished at how different their lives are today. Activists and writers Jennifer Baumgardner and Amy Richards recall what it was like for women in that decade:

> Babies [are] automatically given their father's name. If no father is listed, "illegitimate" is likely to be typed on the birth certifi-cate. There are virtually no child care centers. . . . In high school, the principal is a man. Girls have physical education class [but cannot play] soccer, track, or cross country; nor do they have any varsity sports teams. [The] Miss America Pageant is the biggest source of scholarship money for women. Women can't be students at Dartmouth, Columbia, Harvard, West Point, Boston College, or the Citadel, among other all-male institutions. . . . Only 2 percent of everybody in the military is female, and these women are mostly nurses. . . . [A] married woman can't obtain credit without her husband's signature. She doesn't have her own credit rating, legal domicile [residence], or even her own [maiden] name, unless she goes to court to get it back.[66]

Most of the achievements that changed these old realities did not occur as part of a large-scale legislative bill or a single organized effort by reformers. Rather, they happened on a piecemeal basis over time and as a result of the efforts of a wide range of reformers, organizations, and laws. Historian Ellen Fitzpatrick writes:

> These achievements reflect the increasing power women have amassed [variously] through special interest groups, their rising standing in the major political parties, and [making individual demands for reform based on] the widespread awareness of [women's issues] advanced by feminism in the late 1960s, and 1970s.[67]

Threats to Society and Tradition?

This continuing struggle to improve the status and rights of American women remains a slow, though steady, process. A major reason that it occurs at what some feminists have complained is a very gradual rate is that social change of any kind always has its opponents. In every era, large segments of society tend to resist attempts to modify accepted traditions, especially when those modifications seem at first glance to be too radical.

A majority of feminists feel that this is why opposition to the ERA was so great. In their view, some Americans felt threatened by the empowerment of women. They worried that the amendment would bring about social changes that might adversely affect traditional morality and the established social order. Such worries for society's well-being are illustrated by the writings of the late Baptist preacher Jerry Falwell, who amassed a large following of concerned Americans in the 1980s and 1990s. He condemned both the ERA and the modern women's movement itself as threats to both society and Christian tradition, saying:

> Feminists are saying that self-satisfaction is more important than the family. Most of the women who are leaders in the feminist movement promote an immoral life style. In a drastic departure from the home, more than half of the women in our country are currently employed. Our nation is in serious danger when motherhood is considered a task that is "unrewarding, unfulfilling, and boring." I believe that a woman's calling to be a wife and mother is the highest calling in the world. . . . The Equal Rights Amendment is a delusion. [It] can never do for women what needs to be done for them. Women need . . . a man who knows Jesus Christ as his Lord and Savior, and they need to be part of a home where their husband is a godly leader.[68]

Many Americans agreed with Falwell and other critics of the women's movement. They said that they were

Reverend Jerry Falwell publicly opposed the women's movement in the 1980s and 1990s, citing it as a threat to family values.

not against women's rights to self-expression and fulfillment. Rather, they simply felt that many of the feminists' demands and proposed reforms were too radical. Few doubt that these sentiments were partially responsible for the ERA's ultimate defeat, as well as for strong opposition to numerous other female gender reforms advocated in the decades that followed.

Yet women persevered. Despite many obstacles, they managed to improve their social status, even when their advances were slow and incremental. This hap-

pened in part because they sometimes explored new ways of making themselves heard and instigating change. As University of Wisconsin historian Nancy MacLean tells it:

Feminist organizing continued and even reached into new [social] arenas. As the direct action phase of the movement waned, women brought feminist ideas into the range of institutions that made up American society and reshaped them. . . . A cohort [regiment] of younger women set out to update feminism to meet the challenge of new conditions. The first generation born in the wake of the women's movement's greatest victories came of age in the 1990s, when the contradictions of the women's movement's unfinished revolution were startlingly apparent in American life. They focused on issues of pressing concern to them, such as . . . self-image, diversity, [the] balance [between work and family, and] voter registration campaigns to draw young women into politics.[69]

More Women in the Political Arena

The last issue MacLean mentions—drawing more women into the political arena—turned out to be a crucial step toward female equality.

The earliest significant example occurred in 1984. New York lawyer Geraldine Ferraro became the first woman nominated for vice president by a major party when the Democrats chose her as the running mate to Walter Mondale (who opposed Ronald Reagan for the presidency).

Although the Democrats lost the election, Ferraro's candidacy became a

Allow Women to Utilize Their Talents

In answer to Jerry Falwell and other Christian men who are opposed to the idea of women's equality, evangelical feminist author Letha Scanzoni argues that not allowing women to reach their full potential hurts rather than helps society.

For some women, full-time homemaking is career enough [and] they should never be made to feel guilty for wanting to spend those years in child-rearing and making the home happy and comfortable for the whole family. [However], for other women, full-time homemaking doesn't use their particular talents to the full. Why should they be made to feel guilty about that? Why shouldn't they be encouraged to put their talents to work where they can *best* be used? All of us would be better off—the Church, the society, the women themselves, and yes, their husbands and children. Wanting to develop one's self fully and use talents shouldn't be equated with selfishness. The person who feels fulfilled as a human being—man or woman—is going to have much more to offer others than he or she would have if blocked from that fulfillment.

Letha Scanzoni, "How to Live with a Liberated Wife," *Christianity Today*, June 4, 1976, pp. 7–8.

The four women who serve as justices on the U.S. Supreme Court gather in Washington, D.C., in October 2010; from left: Sandra Day O'Connor, Sonia Sotomayor, Ruth Bader Ginsburg, and Elena Kagan.

symbol of changing times for women in politics. More and more women were inspired to run for public offices of all kinds. Some lost their races. But increasing numbers won them, a trend that culminated in 1992, which became known as the "Year of the Woman." More female candidates were elected that year than in any prior year. They included nineteen congresswomen, rais-

ing the number of women in the House of Representatives to forty-seven; and three senators, bringing the number of females in the Senate to seven. One of these new senators, Carol Moseley Braun, was the first black woman ever to serve in the Senate.

These political gains set the stage for even more stunning triumphs for women in the two decades that followed. In 2007 congresswoman Nancy Pelosi of California became the sixtieth and first female speaker of the House of Representatives. That put her second, after the vice president, in the line of succession that the system activated in the event the president cannot finish his term in office.

The following year, Democrat Hillary Rodham Clinton of New York became the first woman to win a presidential primary (in New Hampshire). Running against her fellow Democratic candidates, she received an impressive 18 million votes in the primary season. Although Barack Obama narrowly defeated her and went on to be elected the first African American president, he appointed Clinton to the prestigious post of secretary of state early in 2009. Meanwhile, during the same presidential election, Sarah Palin, governor of Alaska, was the first woman nominated for vice president by the Republican Party (running with Senator John McCain, who lost to Obama).

Strides were also made by women in appointed government positions, most notably the Supreme Court. In 1981 President Reagan nominated Arizona judge Sandra Day O'Connor to the high court, and the U.S. Senate confirmed her unanimously. She provided the swing vote in many cases, making her one of the most influential of the nine justices on the court. Other female appointments to the Supreme Court followed. They include Ruth Bader Ginsburg, nominated in 1993; Sonia Sotomayor in 2009; and Elena Kagan in 2010. When Kagan took her seat on the court, for the first time in history it featured three women, making up a third of the justices.

A divide remained between men and women in America, however, as evidenced by a widely publicized incident involving the appointment process for the Supreme Court. In 1991 Clarence Thomas of Georgia was nominated to the court by President George H.W. Bush. During Thomas's confirmation hearings, Anita Hill, a law professor at the University of Oklahoma, accused him of sexually harassing her when she had earlier worked for him. The angry Thomas testified that the allegation was untrue. Neither he nor Hill could prove that the other was lying, yet the Senate voted 52 to 48 to confirm his nomination to the high court. Large numbers of women were upset over both the hearing and the confirmation. They felt the incident showed clearly that the existing political system was still an "old boys' club" in which a man's word was almost always taken over a woman's.

Military Women Break Barriers

Whether or not Hill's charges against Thomas were true, overall barriers against women were still falling. One area in which women's strides were particularly dramatic in the 1990s and the decade that followed was the military, "the most avidly masculine major institution in American life," as one prominent feminist puts it. She adds:

Participants in the Defense Advisory Committee on Women in the Armed Forces pressed [the Defense Department] successfully to integrate the armed forces [with female soldiers] and make the [military authorities] act on sexual harassment and other forms of discrimination against servicewomen. The changes proved especially important to African American women and Latinas, who enlist in the military in large numbers in hopes of education funding and social mobility.[70]

A U.S. Marine Corps recruit participates in a boot camp training exercise. The role of women in the U.S. military continues to grow.

The effects of the increased enlistment by young women were dramatic. In the 1991 Persian Gulf War, women made up about 7 percent of the active military forces, more than three times the proportion in 1970. Moreover, 17 percent of the reserve and National Guard forces were women in 1991. In all, more than 40,000 women served in combat support positions in the war, and 16 were killed performing their duties. The wars in Iraq and Afghanistan utilized even more female soldiers. Some 235,000 women served between 2001 and 2010, and an undetermined number actually took part in combat despite military rules prohibiting it. Also by 2010 the proportion of women in the armed forces had doubled to 14 percent, most of them regular soldiers rather than nurses (as had once been the case).

The schooling and training of female soldiers underwent striking changes in the same period. In 1996 the Citadel, in South Carolina, one of the six leading military colleges in the United States, opened its doors to women for the first time. The first woman to graduate from that prestigious military institution was Nancy Mace in 1999. Still another military gender barrier broken was the promotion of Ann Dunwoody of New York to four-star U.S. Army general, the first American woman ever to achieve that esteemed rank.

Advances in the Workplace

The 1980s and the two decades that followed also witnessed some advances by American women in the workplace.

By 2010 women made up a remarkable 46 percent of the total U.S. labor force. In all, 75 percent of adult women were employed outside the home, including an estimated 60 percent of mothers whose children were not of school age.

In sheer numbers, working women's gains were impressive. Also, their jobs proved essential to tens of millions of American families that could not survive, or would be much less comfortable, unless both the husband and wife produced incomes. However, some serious obstacles to working women remained.

One was that child care remained expensive for mothers who either desired to work or were forced to do so by economic pressures. They paid between five thousand and ten thousand dollars a year, per child, for child care services. This often used up a third or more of their wages.

In addition, with a few notable exceptions, women still did not receive completely equal pay. In 2010 American women made, on average, between seventy-five and eighty cents for every dollar earned by a man doing the same job. The rate was even lower for minority women—sixty-four cents for African American women and fifty-two cents for Hispanic women.

The plight of women who suffered from wage discrimination was well illustrated by the case of Lilly Ledbetter, a supervisor at a Goodyear tire plant in Alabama. In 1999 she sued the company, alleging that it paid her 15 percent less than it did men performing the exact same duties. A jury awarded her

Ordeal at the Citadel

The admission of women to the Citadel, in South Carolina, did not come easily. In the early 1990s a young woman named Shannon Faulkner applied to the school without revealing that she was female. Officials accepted her application, saying she was an ideal candidate. Only when they discovered her gender did they change their minds. Faulkner went to court and after a bitter legal battle won admittance to the school in 1995. However, several of her male classmates proved less decent and honorable than she had assumed they would be. She was severely harassed, received death threats, and became so ill she had to withdraw after only a week. Many of the cadets openly celebrated her departure. Reacting to what many Americans saw as a shameful display, she said that she felt "embarrassed for the school" and added, "That's not the school that I wanted to be a part of." In spite of her ordeal, the courageous Faulkner paved the way for others. Since that time more than two hundred women have graduated from the Citadel, several with honors and most without incident.

Quoted in Juju Chang et al., "Life After the Citadel: Shannon Faulkner Reflects on Her Historic Battle with the Elite Military College," December 8, 2009. http://abcnews.go.com/GMA/shannon-faulkner-reflects-citadel/story?id=9272864.

Shannon Faulkner (third from left), the first woman to attend the Citadel, marches with other cadets on their first day at the school in 1995.

Lilly Ledbetter became a key figure in women's quest for equal pay when her 1999 case against her employer went before the Supreme Court.

$224,000 in back pay and more than $3 million in punitive damages. However, Goodyear appealed the verdict. The case eventually went to the Supreme Court, which ruled against Ledbetter, citing a law that stipulated that she should have filed the discrimination charges no later than 180 days following her first inequi- table paycheck. Fortunately for her and other women workers, in 2009 President Barack Obama signed into law the Lilly Ledbetter Fair Pay Act, named in her honor. It allows women, and men too, to sue an employer up to 180 days after *any* inequitable paycheck rather than only the first one.

"No End in Sight"

Recent decades have witnessed improvements for women in more than politics, the military, and employment. A great many of the changes in women's lives have been "small but significant," historian Ruth Rosen points out. For instance, meteorologists came to name hurricanes after both men and women, removing the traditional association of violent natural events with women only. In addition, she says:

Schoolchildren learned about sexism before they became teenagers; language became more gender-neutral; popular culture saturated society with comedies, thrillers, and mysteries that [revolved around] changing gender roles; [and] the number of female lawyers, judges . . . and doctors [increased substantially].[71]

All of these facts and figures show that American women are still advancing, in a number of ways continuing the positive work of their mothers, grandmothers, and great-grandmothers. Although they have still not achieved

Hillary's Story

This brief biography of Secretary of State Hillary Rodham Clinton comes from the U.S. Department of State.

Secretary Clinton was born in Chicago, Illinois on October 26, 1947 to Dorothy Rodham and the late Hugh Rodham. She attended local public schools before graduating from Wellesley College and Yale Law School, where she met Bill Clinton. In 1974, Secretary Clinton moved to Arkansas, a year later then married Bill Clinton and became a successful attorney while also raising their daughter, Chelsea. [In] 1992, Governor Clinton was elected President of the United States, and as First Lady, Hillary Clinton became an advocate of health care reform and worked on many issues relating to children and families. . . . She also traveled to more than 80 countries . . . winning respect as a champion of human rights, democracy and civil society. In 2000, Hillary Clinton made history as the first First Lady elected to the United States Senate. . . . In the Senate she served on the Armed Services Committee [and several other committees]. In 2007 she began her historic campaign for President [and] in November [2009] she was nominated by President-elect [Barack] Obama to be Secretary of State.

U.S. Department of State, "Biography of Hillary Rodham Clinton." www.state.gov/r/pa/ei/biog/115321.htm.

equality with men in every social, political, and economic area, the trend suggests that they will inevitably accomplish that goal. Echoing the positive view of most experts, Rosen offers the following prediction: "The struggle for women's human rights has just begun. As each generation shares its secrets, women learn to see the world through their own eyes, and discover, much to their surprise, that they are not the first, and that they are not alone. [A] revolution is under way, and there is no end in sight."[72]

Notes

Introduction: Working Toward the American Dream

1. Robert S. Fletcher, *History of Oberlin College from Its Foundation Through the Civil War*, vol. 1. Oberlin, OH: Oberlin College Press, 1943, p. 291.
2. Elizabeth K. Minnich, "Education," in *The Reader's Companion to U.S. Women's History*, eds. Wilma Mankiller et al. Boston: Houghton Mifflin, 1998, p. 166.
3. Arthur M. Schlesinger, *New Viewpoints in American History*. New York: Macmillan, 1922, p. 126.
4. Elizabeth L. Kennedy, "Women's Studies," in *The Reader's Companion to U.S. Women's History,* eds, Wilma Mankiller et al. Boston: Houghton Mifflin, 1998, p. 651.
5. Sara M. Evans, *Born for Liberty: A History of Women in America*. New York: Free Press, 1989, p. 314.

Chapter One: The Ordeal of Early American Women

6. Quoted in J.K. Hosmer, ed., *John Winthrop's Journal, 1630–1649*, vol. 2. New York: Scribner's, 1908, p. 239.
7. Eleanor Flexner and Ellen Fitzpatrick, *Century of Struggle: The Women's Rights Movement in the United States*. Cambridge, MA: Harvard University Press, 1996, p. 8.
8. Quoted in Willaim Byrd, *A Journey in the Land of Eden, and Other Papers.* New York: Macy-Masius, 1928, pp. 318–19.
9. David F. Hawke, *Everyday Life in Early America*. New York: Harper and Row, 1989, pp. 63–64.
10. Elizabeth G. Speare, *Life in Colonial America*. New York: Random House, 1963, p. 69.
11. Quoted in Early Americas Digital Archive, "To My Dear and Loving Husband," Maryland Institute for Technology in the Humanities. www.mith2.umd.edu/eada/html/display.php?docs=bradstreet_tomydear.xml&action=show.
12. Jean-Jacques Rousseau, *A Treatise on Education*, ed. William H. Paine. New York: D. Appleton, 1906, p. 263.
13. Hannah Mather Crocker, *Observations on the Real Rights of Women*. Boston, printed for the author, 1818, p. 41.
14. Frances Wright, *Course of Popular Lectures*. New York: Office of the *Free Enquirer*, 1829, p. 44.
15. Quoted in "Fanny Wright," Spartacus Educational. www.spartacus.schoolnet.co.uk/REwright.htm.
16. Quoted in "Fanny Wright," Spartacus Educational.

Chapter Two: Women Learn How to Organize

17. Flexner and Fitzpatrick, *Century of Struggle*, p. 38.

18. Shirley J. Yee, "Abolitionist Movement," in *The Reader's Companion to U.S. Women's History*, Mankiller et al., p. 3.

19. Quoted in Gilbert Barnes and Dwight L. Dumond, eds., *The Letters of Theodore Weld, Angelina Grimke Weld and Sarah Grimke, 1822–1844*, vol. 1. Gloucester, MA: Peter Smith, 1965, p. 430.

20. Quoted in Free Library, "Harriet Beecher Stowe." http://stowe.the freelibrary.com.

21. Quoted in Philip S. Foner, ed., *Selections from the Writings of Frederick Douglass*. New York: International, 1971, p. 86.

22. Elizabeth Cady Stanton et al., eds., *The History of Woman Suffrage*, vol. 1. New York: Fowler's and Wells, 1881, p. 67.

23. Elizabeth Cady Stanton and Susan B. Anthony Papers Project, "Address by Elizabeth Cady Stanton on Women's Rights," Rutgers, the University of New Jersey. http://ecssba.rutgers .edu/docs/ecswoman1.html.

24. Elizabeth Cady Stanton, "Declaration of Sentiments and Resolutions," Feminism and Women's Studies. http://feminism.eserver.org/ history/docs/seneca-falls.txt.

25. Stanton, "Declaration of Sentiments and Resolutions."

26. Flexner and Fitzpatrick, *Century of Struggle*, p. 72.

27. Bonnie Eisenberg and Mary Ruthsdotter, "Living the Legacy: The Women's Rights Movement, 1848–1998," National Women's History Project. www.legacy98.org/move-hist.html.

28. Quoted in Ida H. Harper, *The Life and Work of Susan B. Anthony*. Indianapolis: Bowen-Merrill, 1899, p. 78.

29. Quoted in Brenda Stalcup, ed., *Opposing Viewpoints: The Women's Movement*. San Diego: Greenhaven, 1996, p. 85.

30. Quoted in Harriet Sigerman, "An Unfinished Battle, 1848–1865," in *No Small Courage: A History of Women in the United States*, ed. Nancy F. Cott. New York: Oxford University Press, 2000, p. 279.

31. Quoted in Joel Myerson et al., eds., *The Journals of Louisa May Alcott*. Athens: University of Georgia Press, 1997, p. 27.

32. Quoted in Steven A. Channing, *Confederate Ordeal: The Southern Home Front*. Alexandria, VA: Time-Life, 1984, p. 43.

33. James Dunn, "The Angel of the Battlefield," undated newspaper clipping, in *Clara Barton Papers*, Library of Congress, Washington, D.C.

34. Quoted in Barbara M. Wertheimer, *We Were There: The Story of Working Women in America*. New York: Pantheon, 1997, p. 143.

35. Sigerman, "An Unfinished Battle," in *No Small Courage*, Cott, p. 303.

Chapter Three: The Long Road to the Ballot Box

36. Harriet Sigerman, "Laborers for Liberty, 1865–1890," in *No Small Courage*, Cott, p. 295.

37. Quoted in Flexner and Fitzpatrick, *Century of Struggle*, p. 138.

38. Quoted in Kate Millet, *Sexual Politics.* Urbana: University of Illinois Press, 2000, p. 69.
39. Quoted in Elizabeth Frost and Kathryn Cullen-Dupont, eds., *Women's Suffrage in America: An Eyewitness History.* New York: Facts On File, 1992, p. 202.
40. Quoted in Wertheimer, *We Were There*, p. 68.
41. Quoted in Wertheimer, *We Were There*, p. 272.
42. Quoted in Alice Henry, *Women in the Labor Movement.* New York: George H. Doran, 1923, p. 113.
43. Kathleen M. Blee, "Antifeminism," in *The Reader's Companion to U.S. Women's History*, Mankiller et al., p. 32.
44. Quoted in Sara H. Graham, *Women Suffrage and the New Democracy.* New Haven: Yale University Press, 1996, p. 106.
45. Deborah G. Felder, *A Century of Women.* Secaucus, NJ: Carol, 1999, p. 102.
46. Quoted in Frost and Cullen-Dupont, *Women's Suffrage in America*, p. 336.

Chapter Four: Emergence of the New Public Woman

47. Sarah J. Deutsch, "From Ballots to Breadlines, 1920–1940," in *No Small Courage*, Cott, p. 424.
48. Evans, *Born for Liberty*, p. 175.
49. Evans, *Born for Liberty*, p. 185.
50. Elise Hill and Florence Kelley, "Shall Women Be Equal Before the Law?," *Nation*, April 12, 1922, p. 419.
51. Quoted in William Dudley, ed., *Opposing Viewpoints: The Great Depression.* San Diego: Greenhaven, 1994, p. 36.

52. Quoted in Robert McElvaine, *The Great Depression: America 1929–1941.* New York: Random House, 1993, p. 182.
53. Felder, *A Century of Women*, p. 143.

Chapter Five: Rising Demands for Gender Equality

54. Elaine T. May, "Pushing the Limits, 1940–1961," in *No Small Courage*, Cott, p. 491.
55. May, "Pushing the Limits," p. 492.
56. Evans, *Born for Liberty*, p. 253.
57. Quoted in Cynthia E. Harrison, "A New Frontier for Women: The Public Policy of the Kennedy Administration," *Journal of American History*, vol. 67, December 1980, pp. 641–42.
58. Quoted in Judith Hole and Ellen Levine, *Rebirth of Feminism.* New York: Quadrangle, 1971, p. 84.
59. Quoted in Sara Ruddick and Pamela Daniels, eds., *Working It Out: 23 Women Writers, Artists, Scientists, and Scholars Talk About Their Lives and Work.* New York: Pantheon, 1977, p. 145.
60. Quoted in Edith Mayo and Jerry K. Frye, "The ERA: Post-Mortem of a Failure in Political Communication," in *Rights of Passage: The Past and Future of the ERA*, ed. Joan Hoff-Wilson. Bloomington: University of Indiana Press, 1986, p. 85.
61. Quoted in Jane J. Manbridge, *Why We Lost the ERA.* Chicago: University of Chicago Press, 1986, p. 104.
62. *New York Times*, January 31, 1970, p. 1.

63. John Mack Carter, "The New Feminism," *Ladies Home Journal*, vol. 87, August 1970, pp. 63–64.

64. Quoted in Nancy MacLean, ed., *The American Women's Movement, 1945–2000*. New York: St. Martin's, 2009, p. 114.

65. Evans, *Born for Liberty*, pp. 291–92.

Chapter Six: A Continuing Fight for Status and Rights

66. Jennifer Baumgardener and Amy Richards, *Manifesta: Young Women, Feminism, and the Future*. New York: Farrar, Straus and Giroux, 2000, pp. 315–20.

67. Flexner and Fitzpatrick, *Century of Struggle*, pp. 327–28.

68. Jerry Falwell, "Rise Up Against the Tide of Permissiveness and Moral Decay," in *The American Women's Movement*, MacLean, pp. 148–49.

69. MacLean, *The American Women's Movement*, pp. 36, 41.

70. MacLean, *The American Women's Movement*, p. 38.

71. Ruth Rosen, *The World Split Open: How the Modern Women's Movement Changed America*. New York: Viking, 2000, pp. 338–39.

72. Rosen, *The World Split Open*, p. 344.

For More Information

Books

Deborah G. Felder, *A Century of Women*. Secaucus, NJ: Carol, 1999. A straightforward examination of more than seventy key events in the social and legal evolution of American women.

Eleanor Flexner and Ellen Fitzpatrick, *Century of Struggle: The Women's Rights Movement in the United States*. Cambridge, MA: Harvard University Press, 1996. One of the best available general overviews of the subject.

Jeff Hill, *Women's Suffrage*. Detroit: Omnigraphics, 2006. Aimed at students and general readers, this is a well-researched compilation of information about women's efforts to gain the right to vote, including useful short biographies of the major participants.

Darlene C. Hine and Kathleen Thompson, *A Shining Thread of Hope: The History of Black Women in America*. New York: Broadway, 1998. This well-written, comprehensive look at the history of African American women is a useful companion to general studies of modern women's issues.

Nancy MacLean, ed., *The American Women's Movement, 1945–2000*. New York: St. Martin's, 2009. A collection of essays by experts on the modern women's movement.

Wilma Mankiller et al., eds., *The Reader's Companion to U.S. Women's History*. Boston: Houghton Mifflin, 1998. A comprehensive but easy-to-read collection of short articles on numerous aspects of women's issues and history.

Sally G. McMillen, *Seneca Falls and the Origins of the Women's Rights Movement*. New York: Oxford University Press, 2008. A well-written account of the first few decades of the U.S. women's movement.

John C. Miller, *The First Frontier: Life in Colonial America*. Lanham, MD: University Press of America, 1986. A thoughtful and useful look at life and customs in colonial America, featuring numerous colorful primary source quotations.

Ruth Rosen, *The World Split Open: How the Modern Women's Movement Changed America*. New York: Viking, 2000. An easy-to-read and informative synopsis of the modern women's movement.

Nancy J. Rosenbloom, *Women in American History Since 1880: A Documentary Reader*. New York: Wiley-Blackwell, 2010. An excellent collection of original documents pertaining to women's issues in America.

Barbara M. Wertheimer, *We Were There: The Story of Working Women in*

America. New York: Pantheon, 1997. An informative study of women workers, their work conditions, and their labor organizations, including those of the Industrial Revolution period.

Websites

Clara Barton (http://clarabartonbirth place.org/site). Sponsored by Barton's Birthplace Museum, this site contains links to articles about the famous Civil War nurse and founder of the American Red Cross.

History of Women's Suffrage (http://teacher.scholastic.com/activities/suffrage/history.htm). Provides a short synopsis of the women's suffrage movement, along with some links to related topics.

National Women's Hall of Fame (www.greatwomen.org/home.php). Contains short biographies of hundreds of prominent American women throughout the country's history. To find a person, click on "Women of the Hall," then on the letter corresponding to the first letter of her last name.

Salem Witchcraft Trials, 1692 (www.law.umkc.edu/faculty/projects/ftrials/salem/salem.htm). Contains numerous articles and related information about one of the most disturbing episodes for women in American history.

The Seneca Falls Convention (www.america.gov/st/peopleplace-english/2005/June/20080229183432liameruoy0.6444055.html). A brief overview of the convention and its importance in the history of women in the United States.

The Triangle Factory Fire (www.ilr.cornell.edu/trianglefire/narrative1.html). A multifaceted source of information about one of the worst industrial disasters in U.S. history.

Women's Role Before and During the Colonial Period (www.webconnections.com/MES5th/ColonialWomen_B4.htm). An informative look at colonial women, with numerous photos of modern women in authentic colonial costumes.

Index

Picture Credits

About the Author

In addition to his acclaimed volumes on the ancient world, historian Don Nardo has written and edited many books for young adults about modern European and American history, including *The Age of Colonialism*, *The French Revolution*, *The Atlantic Slave Trade*, *The Declaration of Independence*, *The Great Depression*, and *World War II in the Pacific*. Nardo also writes screenplays and teleplays and composes music. He lives with his wife, Christine, in Massachusetts.